MY
TODDLER

Other Books in the Minirth Meier
New Life Clinic Series

For general information about Minirth Meier New Life Clinic branch offices, counseling services, educational resources, and hospital programs, call toll-free 1-800-NEW-LIFE.

MY TODDLER

THE BEGINNING OF INDEPENDENCE

Dr. Paul Warren

A JANET THOMA BOOK

THOMAS NELSON PUBLISHERS
Nashville • Atlanta • London • Vancouver

Published in Nashville, Tennessee, by Thomas Nelson, Inc., Publishers, and distributed in Canada by Word Communications, Ltd., Richmond, British Columbia.

The Bible version used in this publication is THE NEW KING JAMES VERSION. Copyright © 1979, 1980, 1982, 1990 Thomas Nelson, Inc., Publishers.

Anecdotes and case histories included in this volume are either hypothetical examples or composites of actual cases with names and details changed to protect identities.

Library of Congress Cataloging-in-Publication Data

Warren, Paul, 1949–
    My toddler : the beginning of independence / Paul Warren.
        p.   cm. — (The stepping-stones series for Christian parents)
    ISBN 0-7852-8347-1
    1. Toddlers. 2. Child rearing. 3. Parenting—Religious aspects—
Christianity. I. Title. II. Series.
HQ774.5.W38 1994
649′.122—dc20   94–33807
                                                                    CIP

Printed in the United States of America.
1 2 3 4 5 6 — 99 98 97 96 95 94

To my wife, Vicky,
whose love of children
reminds me of God's love for children,
and to my son, Matthew,
whose love teaches and encourages me.

CONTENTS

Children are our most valuable
natural resource.

HERBERT HOOVER

ACKNOWLEDGMENTS

The author acknowledges the vision and direction of Janet Thoma, vice president of Thomas Nelson Publishers. Sandy Dengler's creativity made the manuscript come alive. Amy Glass's and Sue Ann Jones's careful editing kept the manuscript crisp and clear.

1. BECOMING A PERSON

PHYSICAL DEVELOPMENT

Growth is the only evidence of life.

JOHN HENRY NEWMAN

Party animal! Yeah, yeah! His one-year birthday party, and how Brian loved it! True, the guests—relatives and friends of Mommy and Daddy—were all a whole lot older, but he didn't care. Not only had Tom and Marsha Jasper married late, they had tried for five years to have children. Their friends' youngest children, therefore, were considerably bigger than Brian.

No problem. The big kids doted on this charming baby, laughing at him, playing with him, fighting over the privilege of changing him. And did Brian relish the attention? Do clowns dress up?

His favorite present seemed to be a plastic indoor slide from his aunt and uncle. Over and over, he entertained himself by climbing the steps and sliding down. A couple of other children tried it and found it boring. In a matter of months, so would Brian.

What to Expect

Progress at Brian's age must be measured in months and weeks, for it occurs quickly, change upon change.

Physically, from birth to one year, a child changes more profoundly in a briefer space of time than at any other stage of development. But this second-year toddler time is also a period of intense change.

Even though on the outside a child doesn't seem to change as much during toddlerhood, a lot of new things go on beneath the surface. Marsha and Tom had much to look forward to. Even though it would slow dramatically, their child's physical growth—size, coordination, and mobility—would serve as the vehicle for all other aspects of his development—social progress, intelligence, language, and that evasive, indefinable thing called the whole child. How well Brian developed physically would also strongly determine how well he would grow intellectually, emotionally, and socially.

Developmental psychologists are just now recognizing how crucial these beginning years are. Unfortunately, by and large, society hasn't quite caught the drift. Because children don't begin, until about the age of six or so, to achieve measurable results such as grades, sports talent, or success with a hobby, it may appear that they're not accomplishing much.

Nothing could be farther from the truth. The first three years make the child, quite literally. During these years the child lays the foundation on which every later experience and every later choice will be based. Should that foundation prove inadequate, three things may happen. First, the individual will experience childhood difficulties, friction, and problems. It won't be easy on the child's family either, of course. Second, the child/adult will be unable to build satisfying, lasting relationships and may engage in self-destructive behavior. Third, change will come only if the adult child chooses to change, and even then, change will not be easy.

There are clear ways we, as childcare experts and parents, can build a strong foundation for children, and frankly, there are ways in which we can weaken the foundation. For better or worse, toddlerhood offers a unique window of opportunity to build or to tear down.

Physical development offers the easiest indication of growth, of course. But it is not sheer weight gain. In fact, children gain much less weight per month during their second year of life than their first. The average one-year-old puts on something like eight ounces to one pound every two months; an infant grows at a rate of one-fourth to half a pound per week.

The child's shape changes subtly but perceptibly as well. At the beginning of this second year, the physical build of the Jaspers' toddler is suited for life on all fours. He has a comparatively large head, a round tummy that would do Santa Claus proud, a stocky neck, and short, stubby arms and legs. Toward the middle of his second year his body will gradually elongate into a physique more suited to a pedestrian life on two long legs. By the time his second birthday rolls around, even though his increase in sheer size will be modest, he will have lengthened out into a longer-limbed version of a toddler, closer in proportion to the shape we associate with preschoolers. A child is two years old before his arms are long enough and his skull proportionally small enough to permit him to clap his hands together above his head.

Let's summarize some of the developmental milestones showing up about now, always remembering that toddlers each have their own individual timetables. However, two very important characteristics, curiosity and exploration, should be evident in this second year. If they are not, you may wish to discuss the matter with your pediatrician.

Once that first birthday passes, what might you expect?

Twelve to Eighteen Months

As he celebrated his first birthday, Brian was preoccupied with mastering his new motor skills, particularly climbing and walking. He drove Marsha nuts. Children of this age are fascinated by stairs. Hinged objects such as cupboards and doors hold special interest for a one-year-old.

"Brian spends hours simply opening and shutting a cabinet door," claimed Marsha, exaggerating only by a magnitude or two.

For the same reason, one-year-olds love stiff-paged books, called board books, because they can turn the pages themselves. Picking up small objects is enjoyable for a one-year-old. Any such object will immediately go into the mouth, however, so make certain you find swallowable things before the child does. One mother, worried that her toddler wasn't eating enough, capitalized on her child's small-object fascination at this age by leaving bits of food lying about. As we'll discuss later, subconsciously this was more of a control issue on the mother's part than a nutrition concern. And it certainly doesn't help the child learn *not* to put objects in his or her mouth.

There is a difference in what you might call the philosophy of physical activity between small children and older ones. Ten-year-olds engage in physical activity primarily for the pleasure of the activity itself. They swing on the swing because they simply love to swing on the swing. They ride their bikes, not just to get somewhere, but to be out on the road. To the one-plus-year-old, however, the pleasure of physical play is not so much the activity itself as the joy of mastering the skill. Thus, on his first birthday, Brian loved his little plastic slide—climbing up those stairs, getting seated, sliding down. Once he learned to do it well, though, it ceased to be a challenge and he abandoned the slide (much to his parents' relief; that toy took up a large patch of living-room space).

The child this age will, in general, come across as a friendly, happy kid . . . with intense preferences. One of those preferences will be for the primary caretaker. Kids twelve to eighteen months old will feel much more comfortable around strangers if the strangers are in the kids' home.

Curiosity is a powerful motivating force during this period of a child's life and a necessary one, for it drives the child to explore. By the age of one, most children have adult-level capabilities in hearing and eyesight.

Eighteen Months to Two Years

My, how the temperament has changed, from baby to inquisitive toddler. The cheerful little earful is fast becoming an obstinate, negative brat. Your child is learning about others, sorting out the reality that other people out there function independently of him or her (an immensely important lesson that does not come naturally). The child is also beginning to master language skills. Somewhere around the middle of this period, "No!" becomes a favorite word, rife with meaning and attractiveness, sort of like forbidden fruit.

The child is intensely interested in exploring the environment, spending lots of time just looking and listening to what goes on around him or her. Your little one enjoys listening to you talk to others and especially likes it when you talk directly to him or her.

The child might show some mild interest in television, but it will not yet become the hypnotic baby-sitter. Most children don't really watch television, by which I mean derive meaning from it, until near the end of their third year. Your toddler probably loves playing outside and/or playing with water. Swinging is a favorite activity at this age.

Ideally, at about age twenty to twenty-four months, there begins what can be a lifelong love affair with art and writing. If it doesn't happen in this second year of growth, don't worry about it. If it does show up, though, I urge you to encourage it. The first scribbling and drawing attempts, unintelligible to pseudo-sophisticates such as adults, are immensely important experiments in what happens when writing instrument meets paper (or walls, or books . . . supervise!). At this stage the process itself holds sufficient charm to keep the child interested. Indeed, children become so wrapped up in the process that they close out the outside world, and praise and condemnation alike fall on deaf ears. You are aware, of course, that your job is not to critique but to praise.

Along with physical growth and development during the child's second year comes neurological development and agility, coordinated efforts between hand and eye, and between foot and other foot. Part of that coordination includes the heady experience of learning to feed oneself.

At the same time, the toddler's new mobility invites the first real steps of separation and individuation, gaining the understanding that he or she is a human being distinct from all others. In testing this new individuality and finding the boundary lines between himself and others, Brian would engage in an experimental contest of wills with his mommy and daddy. In so doing he would not be acting deliberately perverse. He would be feeling out and defining his universe. Marsha and Tom would not always remember that.

One of the first battlegrounds between Established Authority (that's Tom and Marsha) and the Experimenting Upstart (Brian) is usually in the matter of food. Food and its use is a powerful control issue from now right on through adulthood. Like all party animals, Brian will take delight in what is essentially a long, continuing food fight.

Why Won't My Child Eat?

When she was seventeen, Jenny Lawton made a major, life-changing error, although she did not recognize it as an error at the time. Only when her pregnancy was confirmed and she began to actually see its progress did the full consequences of her error strike her. Understanding at least some of the sacrifices her choice would require, she decided to keep the baby. In due time, little Sara arrived.

Jenny lived with her parents while she finished high school. An entry-level job at a fast-food restaurant seemed right to fill the space between graduation and deciding what her next options were. She paid no rent—her minimum wage wouldn't allow that—but she paid her mom for childcare.

As Sara entered her second year, Jenny bumped into an issue that can cause parents to tear out their prematurely graying hair—their toddlers' eating habits. More specifically, their toddlers' *non*-eating habits. Kids seem to stop eating by the time they reach, say, eighteen months. There are several reasons for this, but they are almost never the reasons parents think.

Jenny did things right; she brought this area of major concern to the attention of her pediatrician during one of Sara's routine appointments. As Sara, wearing a pink-flowered diaper, toddled about the office stiff-legged, staggering from chair to stool to exam table, Jenny told the doctor about her daughter's nonexistent eating habits. "I'm afraid she'll starve, Dr. Brighton. You know, that failure-to-thrive thing. Look how puny she is."

"Petite, yes. Puny, no." Dr. Brighton smiled. She was an older lady of what some would call ample proportions. "She's on the low end of the growth chart, but her size is not nearly as important as her rate of growth. And that is satisfactory. As long as she's gaining, she's doing great. Don't worry about size."

"But what is she gaining *on?*"

One Reason Toddlers Don't Eat

Dr. Brighton chuckled. "Nearly all parents of toddlers complain about their children's eating habits. That's because kids' eating habits always change during this second year. You see, Sara isn't a baby anymore. Since she's not gaining weight as fast as little babies do, she doesn't require anywhere near the calories she did as a baby. Like all of us, she still needs a well-balanced diet. But that doesn't mean she has to have all the basic food groups at every meal. She can get her nutritional needs—meat, potatoes, vegetables, fruit, bread, milk—here and there, by picking."

"That's how she eats, all right. Picking."

Kids love to pick. And yet, until their palates are subverted by sugary foods, little kids are extremely good at meeting their own nutritional needs. In a famous and classic study, babies presented with a variety of finger foods at mealtime somehow managed to balance out their diet over the space of a week or so. They might eat potatoes for three days straight, no meat at all for days, fruit now and then or maybe constantly. In the end, they provided themselves with the necessary array of different kinds of foods.

What are a baby's needs?

Think for a moment what foods do. The body is an extraordinarily complex chemical factory, turning the elaborate chemical compounds of foods into extremely simple compounds, then using those simple compounds to create the equally elaborate chemical compounds that make up the body. This takes two kinds of food, energy sources to keep the factory running and raw materials—building blocks—for repair and growth.

Energy Foods. Adult males who are candidates for cardiac problems are advised to avoid dietary fats. Some people expand that proscription to include babies and toddlers, as if any dietary fat is bad. In toddlers, dietary fat is necessary for healthy brain development. It's the source of building material for the process of *myelination* (that is, brain development) as well as for production of many hormones.

The other ready energy sources are sugars and the more complex compounds derived from them, carbohydrates. Diet-conscious women avoid fats, sugars, and carbohydrates. One-year-olds shouldn't.

Building Components. "Everything that Mrs. Tea eats . . . turns into Mrs. Tea."

Each person's proteins are unique—to the extent that even twins have trouble exchanging body parts. The fact that a body rejects any protein components not its own makes organ transplants a difficult medical undertaking. Salmon protein tastes much different from trout protein, although both fishes are members of the same family, the *Salmonidae*. These unique proteins are fashioned from a few simple components, building blocks called amino acids.

Although every protein is unique, the amino acids are few and universal. By exact analogy, twenty-six letters of the alphabet can be combined to write an infinite number of books, articles, billboards, and letters . . . in several real or manufactured languages.

The body is built of protein. Every structure and organ, including the bones, is protein-based. In the living body, digestion breaks down protein into its component amino acids. All human beings use those amino acids, freed by digestion, to build new protein for repair and growth.

Now not all protein sources are created equal. Some

foods contain all the amino acids—we call them complete proteins—and others lack one or more amino acids. As a rule of thumb, animal sources for protein are complete. Eggs, milk, and meat give children (and adults, for that matter) all the amino acids in good supply. Vegetable sources, such as beans, lack some essential amino acids. But different vegetables lack different amino acids. By mixing vegetables, the lack in one can be made up by another. For example, legumes such as peas or beans are frequently served with rice. Rice is a good source of tryptophan; legumes lack it. Beans are incomplete and rice is incomplete; together, they form a complete protein source. This is probably why so many ethnic dishes combine the two foods, such as red beans and rice—also called hopping John.

"And so," Dr. Brighton concluded, "I suggest that you offer Sara a variety of foods in very small quantities and allow her to pick. As long as she doesn't develop a taste for very sweet foods such as candy, she'll get what she needs. When she's done eating, let her down."

"Wow." Jenny wagged her head. "If you say so, okay. But I don't think Mom's gonna buy it. Mom does everything but stand upside down and stack BBs, trying to get Sara to eat more. Boy, is that kid stubborn!"

"As you were when you were a baby, I'll bet."

Jenny frowned. "Mom says that all the time. How did you know?"

How, indeed, did Dr. Brighton know? And if toddlers are so wise about choosing needed foods over the long run, why don't they eat well?

The Other Reason Toddlers Won't Eat

Dr. Brighton knew Jenny was a picky eater as a toddler because when Jenny mentioned the tussle between Sara and Grandma, a big flag waved. The flag was emblazoned, "Food fight! Control issue ahead!"

Even a child Sara's age can detect an opportunity to see who's boss. This is not simple obstinacy, although it certainly seems so. At a nonverbal level, Sara was asking the questions, *Just how separate am I from Grandma?* and *How strong am I?* So she tried refusing to do what Grandma wanted her to. Grandma's response would be her answer.

When Sara experimentally disobeyed commands to, for example, stay away from the bookcase, she would be physically removed from the problem. The answers to her questions then were, *You are separate, but you are not strong. Grandma's will prevails.*

Ah, but food. The old adage, You can lead a horse to water but you can't make it drink, could be rewritten to say, No one can make a toddler eat if the toddler refuses. When Sara refused to cater to Grandma's will about eating a large (for Sara) quantity, Sara won. The answer, a new and heady realization, became, *You are separate, and you are strong! Even Grandma's iron will cannot prevail!*

The fact that Sara did not actually need the food being forced upon her made this struggle easy for her. However, Grandma had been trained that toddlers need a plateful. Grandma was frustrated. Sara played upon that frustration, again below conscious level, reexperiencing the wonderful message over and over, *You are you, and you are strong.*

How do you prevent food from becoming a control issue of this sort?

Solving and Preventing Eating Problems

Jenny and her parents normally sat down together at the evening meal, with Sara in a high chair between Jenny and her mom. Jenny had rarely coaxed Sara to eat, even before hearing Dr. Brighton's counsel. Mom, though, virtually ruined the family time together by constantly nagging at Sara to take one more little bite. Typically, Jenny's dad stayed out of it, leaving the table as soon as possible to go watch the news before the weather came on.

When Jenny brought Dr. Brighton's comments home from the appointment, her dad agreed heartily right away. He was all for a return to peace and normalcy. Jenny's mom also agreed in principle with Dr. Brighton's position, but she still kept coaxing Sara as much as ever.

Power struggles, you see, are two-sided. One side is the child, asking a question and receiving an answer, and on the other side is the adult who has a need, the need to control. The adult rationalizes: *This is a tiny person, a toddler; surely control is not only possible but necessary.* In this way, the food issue had become a cause célèbre to Sara's mom—bigger than life, an issue she couldn't let go.

In essence, the power struggle would ease when Jenny's mom lightened up and quit forcing. Should she decide to do this, ego would come into play; a voice would scream deep down inside her, *You can't let a little baby win this struggle!* But that would not be the issue at all. Jenny's mom was fighting a battle of her own making, a battle that was not a battle because she could not by any means control that aspect of Sara's life. No way. If you consider this as a win-lose issue, which admittedly is not an acceptable way to look at it, Sara had already won before the battle began.

Besides the obvious, that the swords between Sara and her grandma somehow had to be laid down, there are a number of other things the Lawtons could do to ease food issues and get a maximum amount of nutrition into this active toddler. So can you.

Distinguish Between Mealtime Behavior and Eating Needs. Grandma's need to see Sara sitting still and eating everything put before her differed greatly from Sara's actual nutritional needs. Separating these two issues will minimize any conflicts over food. A toddler's least favorite activity is to sit still. If you want your child to sit at the meal with the rest of the family—an excellent bonding device, incidentally—provide messy foods the baby can play in, things that smear and feel funny. Babies love textures. Capitalize on that. If you can't make a mess when you're a year old, when can you? When interest in food flags, provide a spoon to bang with or a few toys.

Let the Child Eat Whatever in Whatever Combination. "Are you kidding?" Jenny might ask. "Sara dipped her meat in her yogurt and then in her applesauce. Blecch!" Sara might dip her meat in ice cream. No problem; it's nutritious, even if it's not appetizing to adults. Let your toddler have fun experimenting with food combinations.

A word about taste here. Tiny children do possess a sense of taste, but it's not well developed yet. The salt in some commercially prepared baby foods is not there to improve palatability for the child but for the adult who tastes the stuff to test for temperature or flavor. One-year-olds don't respond to strong, appealing flavors nearly as much as older children do . . . which will be a blessing if you let your toddler experiment with mixes.

Provide Foods Your Toddler Can Eat by Himself or Herself. Bite-size portions that your child can handle are perfect. Again, let your toddler explore foods with tactile senses—touchy-feely. A child can have great fun learning to eat, and that is a key to smooth mealtimes—having fun. If you don't have a pet to clean up under the high chair, put down a plastic tablecloth or a split-open garbage bag.

Let the Child Down When Finished, Even If Food Remains. Here is where Grandma fell flattest. If she served a tablespoon of peas, she thought Sara ought to eat a tablespoon of peas. That's when the immovable object met the irresistible force over the question of how much food is enough. Were Jenny to intervene, she would probably have little luck altering the situation, considering her low position on the totem pole. Her father, though, might be able to intervene successfully and see that this guideline was met.

Consider a Separate Mealtime for Your Toddler. Frankly, I don't advocate this because the meal the family eats together is an immensely effective cohesive force, and the toddler is a part of that family. Such meals in which the whole family sits down together are becoming increasingly rare in our helter-skelter society, to our detriment. I mention a separate mealtime for toddlers as an option that some follow, particularly if a little squirmer is disruptive during what is normally a quiet, happy, family time.

Some families, seeking at least one peaceful mealtime a day, serve a separate early meal to the toddler, tuck the child in bed, and proceed with a quiet dinner for the rest of the family. Before you go to that extreme, may I suggest sharing the candlelight and soft music with the youngster. This romantic atmosphere is also a very pacifying one. Children who bounce and fidget under the glare of full lighting may become noticeably quieter when the lights go down and peaceful music fills the background. Peaceful music has a fairly slow beat and a soft, gentle sound. I suggest nonvocal instrumental pieces.

There is an added benefit of dinner music. Many adult music aficionados have told me, "I grew up listening to classical and semiclassical music. It made all the difference in my life."

Should you exercise the option of feeding your young toddler separately, by the age of three he or she ought to be settled enough to join the family meals.

Don't Place Emphasis on Preparing Food for Your Toddler. It's very hard to see a meal that has been lovingly and painstakingly prepared rejected by a crass and picky little toddler. The rejection isn't really rejection in the adult sense, of course, but it hurts anyway. If you prepare foods just for your little one, keep them simple and easy.

There is a corollary here also. If food is glorified and put on a pedestal, a child is bound to take notice and make it an issue. I know families where the elaborate preparation and eating of fancy foods is something on the order

---

of a consuming family hobby. Does that situation pertain in your case? To find out, pretend you are a stranger hanging around the kitchen and dining room during preparation and mealtime. What would your impression be if you were a neutral observer?

Don't Use Food As a Reward or Punishment. What did Grandma hold out as an enticement to Sara for finishing a serving? More food. A cookie or cracker. She also engaged frequently in its corollary of not allowing Sara to have dessert unless she ate everything on her plate. Again, this is a control issue, not an eating issue.

Stop and consider the effect on eating habits of a threat such as, "If you don't quit what you're doing, I'll give you an extra helping of spinach tonight!"

Neither do I recommend withholding dessert from a toddler because of naughty behavior. The key is to avoid tying food to any reward or punishment system. Food should never be a part of discipline.

Don't Worry About Snacks. Babies' digestive systems are geared to frequent little meals. Foods pass quickly through the pipes. A mid-morning, mid-afternoon, or evening snack, therefore, is not going to adversely affect appetite. A nibble at two is gone by five. Sara's grandma can neither improve nor damage her chances of getting Sara to eat more at meals by introducing snacks between meals. Fruit—apple or pear wedges, banana, or *de-seeded* tangerine sections—makes a fine snack. Crackers are fine too. But no candy please.

I am the first to admit that letting picky little eaters have their way grates upon adult sensibilities. After all, we are bigger and stronger. We know what is best. Our desires are for the child's welfare, and the child ought to behave. However, I also see where future eating disorders find their roots in this period of a person's life, when food becomes a power issue between a child and a parent. Girls aged fifteen cannot be forced to eat anymore than girls of one can (if driven to eating they may vomit it later, the disorder called bulimia). Conversely, food cannot be kept away from girls of fifteen if they choose to eat to excess, as some do. They'll find it, sneak it, obtain it.

A little slack cut now, against your better judgment as it were, can avoid far more serious problems later.

Potty Time

Children between the ages of one and two rarely potty train, and the same philosophy—that cutting a little slack now will pay dividends later—applies. Parents often train well, able to see an accident before it happens and take evasive action. But toddlers' sphincters, the muscles controlling the flow of wastes, are not well developed or responsive yet. Small children literally cannot hold it. In fact, as they do potty train, their control will be limited for several years. When they gotta go, they gotta go!

In earlier generations, how early your child was potty trained somehow became a measure of how good a parent you were. I remember a side-view picture in a childcare manual of the thirties or forties of a proud, matronly sort of lady sitting in a chair. On her lap was a little china potty, and on the potty sat her tiny infant. The text suggested that now was the time to familiarize the child with the process.

Unless the child comprehends and, even more important, cares, potty training before age two is a bust. *But:*

By two and a half years, most girls *will* care, and they will potty train fairly quickly and smoothly. Most boys will have the interest and physical control to potty train by three. As soon as a child grasps the idea that he or she is a big kid now, potty training will become a top priority. And once the child ranks it high, it will happen unless, as in a very small number of cases, some physical problem or emotional problem interferes. For now, don't worry about it. Eating is an issue; the potty is not.

Childproofing Your Home

This heading really ought to read "*Partially* Childproofing Your Home." Kids can get into trouble despite their parents' most ardent efforts to remove potential hazards. As I identify some prominent hazards here, I will also review the childproofing that was left over, so to speak, from the previous year.

During their second year, kids become very interested in the most mundane of common household objects—spatulas, dusters, and that most intriguing of utensils, the eggbeater. Now is when peanut-butter sandwiches start showing up in the slot of the VCR. Now is when you must anticipate their inspirations.

Not even Robin Williams is as wildly inventive as the razor-sharp mind of a yearling. In theory, you childproofed your home before the baby began crawling. Now, I suggest you go through the place again, making sure your child's home environment is as safe as a home ought to be.

Pets and Other Animals

The Jaspers owned a gray, tiger-striped cat named Killer and a weimaraner named Dumkopf—Dum for short. Both pets had proven themselves safe with small children. It's an important point to consider when bringing children and animals together. Remember, too, that a little kid is a natural menace to any animal smaller than a pony.

When Brian was an infant, he was too rough to be good with animals. By the time he was walking well, though, he also had the muscle control to be able to pet the cat without flattening it. Coached extensively by Tom and Marsha, he could now be trusted with the family pets, and they could be trusted with him.

But Brian's world of animals was expanding far beyond family pets. He was walking—make that *running*—and coming into contact with many other animals. In the neighborhood were other pets. On a friend's farm, a number of intriguing animals seized his attention. At the park or in the zoo were hosts more.

Compounding Brian's native fascination for animals were Tom and Marsha's worries. Neither of them had grown up around animals other than dogs and cats. What if Brian eluded their supervision temporarily? It happened. What creatures were harmless and what animals lurked, eager to eat their son?

Here are some general rules of thumb—but keep in mind that there are exceptions to every rule:

Horses: Most horses are very good with kids. Even edgy, nervous horses such as thoroughbreds seem to understand to be gentle with tiny children. A wrangler friend relates this tale from a handicapped children's camp where horses were part of the activities. Visiting press photographers wanted a picture of a blind camper on a particularly photogenic horse, which happened to be one of the wildest of the camp's string. With considerable trepidation, my friend boosted the blind girl up on the horse, stationing brawny young men all around to catch her if the dancing animal shook the girl loose.

To quote the wrangler, "That miserable, hot-blooded beast was squirreling around like he was dancing the tango. Constantly in motion. I was holding him by an ear as we boosted little Ella up onto him. He stopped. I mean, he *stopped*. Very smoothly and gently, he took her for the sweetest ride around the lawn as the photographers snapped away. She was laughing and really loving it. I noticed his neck and flanks were wet—nervous sweat. We pulled her down off him and instantly he's dancing around again, sidling and pawing. He knew. Horses always know."

Cattle: Frankly, I wouldn't trust a cow or steer. Most are fine, but some are indifferent and can hurt without trying. You're talking about nearly a thousand pounds on the hoof. Certainly never trust a bull. Should a small child wander into a pasture or enclosure with untrustworthy animals, divert the animal's attention elsewhere; if possible, lure it into another enclosure or building.

Hogs: Large sows—and brood sows can grow to immense size—can be dangerous under certain conditions (if they are not feeling well, are injured in some way, are protecting piglets, etc.). Pigs are intelligent. They can quickly assess a situation and will likely decide that the child is harmless and you are not. So in a hog pen you are in greater potential danger than your child. Farmers control hogs in part by maneuvering a wide plywood board in their faces, thus steering them in the desired direction.

Wild Animals: Although it is strictly illegal, in Yosemite National Park, visitors love to feed snacks to the "wild" deer. And the deer accept such goodies unabashedly. The danger in this situation became apparent when an antlered buck heard a potato chip bag rustle and suddenly turned its head, accidentally puncturing the lung of a five-year-old. Such accidents are exceedingly rare, but they point up the fact that wild animals are indeed wild. Male deer, elk, and moose in particular become truculent in autumn. Never, ever trust Bambi!

In some parts of the country, cougars have been encroaching into suburban areas; more properly, suburban areas have been encroaching into cougar territory. Cat-versus-human incidents have increased. Bears are a similar threat. Rarely aggressive, they can still hurt a child who happens to be blocking an exit or an escape route.

Any small creature—squirrel, chipmunk, marmot, groundhog, ground squirrel, rabbit—that acts strange should be avoided. "Strange" means sluggish, not alert, or nervous, perhaps aggressive, and possessing a dull coat that appears in need of brushing. The animal could be ill, and quite possibly the illness could be contagious—and deadly.

Don't handle bats. They have very, very sharp little teeth.

Obvious Hazards

"I swear, he lies awake at night thinking up dangerous things to do. The 'Perils of Pauline' were nothing compared to Brian. I'm surprised he doesn't tie himself to the railroad track." Marsha paused. "Uh-oh. I don't hear anything." She hurried off in search of her son.

A child younger than two simply does not have the background knowledge or self-control to stay out of trouble. Even when parents reinforce a lesson over and over—"This is dangerous! Stay away!"—the child will be attracted to it. It's not disobedience. The child can't help it.

Sometimes the only course of action is conditioning. This is a situation in which you allow the child to be hurt a little, under carefully supervised circumstances, so that he or she understands the danger. An example might be a woodstove that cannot be fenced away or shielded. The child touches it. The child is burned. The child then avoids it. It's all rather Pavlovian. Conditioning should be a last resort.

Check your home for other possible hazards, including:

Electrical Outlets and Cords. You can purchase protectors to insert into unused outlets so curious children cannot stick pins into them. Duct tape can close them off in a pinch. If extension cords are necessary, make certain the unused outlets at the female end are plugged. Check all cords for breaks or fraying. Never allow a small child to play with extension cords or other electrical items.

Stairs. Once they're older than two, children can handle stairs pretty well, but kids from one to two should be monitored. At the end of the first year, fence off stairs with spring-loaded protective gates. You can probably safely remove them as the child approaches two.

Make sure the vertical bars of stair and balcony railings are close enough together to prevent little heads from getting caught between them. Yes, it certainly does happen frequently. Replace the bars of problem railings.

Cabinets and Their Contents. So many cases of poisoning occur in children under five, and it is all unnecessary! You can purchase latches that fit inside the cabinet doors and keep them from opening more than about an inch. An adult can loosen the latch to swing the door clear open, but small children cannot. Even if the cabinets are secured, don't put poisons in them where children can reach them. Keep anything poisonous or irritating *high*.

Poisons include any caustic cleaning and polishing substances, the obvious stuff such as lye and bleach, medicines, and vitamins. Vitamins? you may ask. Absolutely, vitamins. An adult dose of iron supplement can kill a small child or forever ruin his or her liver function. Keep all such substances out of reach.

Things That Choke. "He stuffs *everything* in his mouth!" Marsha sang the lament of every parent of a child this age.

Marsha's husband, Tom, had come up with an innovative, if not very sophisticated, way to deal with this problem. Marsha grimaced. "I don't agree with Tom's idea, but I have to admit I've used it."

Tom had taught Brian to spit, rewarding him with praise and laughing, positive attention. It was not a pretty thing. Tom called it a man-to-man thing, and Brian doted on it. "Hey, Brian! Spit!" Anything in Brian's mouth at the moment came flying out.

"Gross!" Marsha shuddered. But when Brian unscrewed a cabinet knob and popped it in his mouth, she cried out, "Brian! Spit!" and the knob clattered to the floor.

That cabinet knob brings up another point. A child crawling or just learning to walk is what biologists call an *opportunistic browser.* The child more or less accidentally comes across some small item and mouths it.

Children aged one to two are opportunistic browsers—and a lot more. They have the background knowledge and manual dexterity to *create* small items. They can pull or twist off knobs from electronic equipment and cabinets. They can break off pieces from carvings or large bric-a-brac. Children who will not touch spinach will eagerly chow down on houseplants as well as dirt from the overturned pots. They pull toilet tissue from the roll and can choke on the soggy paper.

Older brothers and sisters ought to put their treasured belongings up high and put away any toys with small parts. Playthings such as Barbie dolls and GI Joes are especially vulnerable; nearly every associated part is swallowable. Siblings should be encouraged to safely stow all toys of value to them, for the toys' safety as well as the toddler's.

When canvassing your house for small items, be aware

of large items possessing small parts. Be particularly protective of electronic equipment such as VCRs, stereos, and CD players. Small children can wreak costly havoc in a hurry.

The Bathroom. If you don't fence off the bathroom, supervise it closely. Children love to play in and on the toilet (not only does it splash, it's climbable), and they can drown if they fall headfirst into the commode. Drowning is a significant cause of death in children under five, and it simply does not have to be.

Swimming Pools. Tragically, many children also drown in swimming pools. Even inflatable backyard pools can be deadly for unsupervised toddlers, and should be empty when not in use. If you have an inground pool, it must be completely enclosed by a secure fence. Make sure all doors and gates leading to the pool are double locked—including a deadbolt lock—and hide the keys! Pool supply stores sell alarms that sound when the water surface is broken. None of these precautions are foolproof. There is no substitute for a vigilant parent.

Vehicles. Children this age can turn window cranks and operate door handles. You'll want to keep the windows closed because children will throw any manner of things out the window, given the opportunity—toys, a bottle, a pet, a shoe . . . Make certain doors are locked whenever the vehicle is in motion. And never ever—never *ever!*—put the vehicle in motion unless the child is correctly secured in an appropriate carseat and the seat is correctly strapped down. Absolutely no haste or inconvenience justifies the tragedy that could occur if the child is unsecured. I repeat, never.

The more you do to create a safe environment, the more peaceful it will be. You can relax more (not totally, but more), and you may conserve some of your energy for the additional challenges of this age . . .

The Inevitable Conflicts

At Sara's next doctor's appointment, Jenny met Shauna Moore, another single mother. Shauna's three-year-old girl, Afton, contented herself with the picture books on the end table. As she watched, a stab of jealousy shot through Jenny before she could catch it. Afton looked so—so mature.

Suddenly very tired of holding her little wiggle-worm, she set Sara down on the floor while she waited for her receipt. Immediately, Sara teetered off toward the toy corner.

"Your first?" Shauna asked Jenny.

"Yeah. And one's enough!"

"Amen! I thought I'd never make it through Afton's terrible twos. Fortunately for my sanity, every year gets a little better."

From the toy corner, a doll came flying.

Jenny nodded, watching the vivid contrast that a year makes. "They change a lot in a hurry."

"So do we." Shauna said, kind of smiling. "I guess I'm learning to be more tolerant or something. And I'm more aware of what to expect now so I can act instead of react. You know?"

"That's what I need—some way to know what's coming. How do you do that?" Jenny watched Sara lurch toward the rest room door.

"Read books, for one. Talk to other moms, like my sister, who have had their kids and been through it all. Some of the women from my church are helpful, too, but they sure don't volunteer anything. You have to ask."

"A woman in our congregation said if I needed something I should call her, but she didn't really sound like she meant it, you know?"

"Oh, they usually do. They just don't know how to talk to unwed mothers, 'specially the older women. So you tell them what you need and ask them. They're happy to help when there's something specific to do."

"I'll remember that." Jenny got up and retrieved Sara to forcibly end her happy game of banging on the rest room door.

Shauna's voice became soft. "About the time Afton hit two, I thought I was going to go nuts. Thank the Lord someone answered my cry for help."

Jenny sat down with her squirming armful. By and large, Sara had been a pretty good baby so far. But little glimpses were occurring now, giving Jenny hints that the immediate future would be vastly different. Things like stubbornness and persistence with forbidden activities were beginning to surface.

She's a lot like me, Jenny thought.

The receptionist stuck her head out into the room. "Afton Moore?"

Shauna stood up and called Afton. She handed a slip of paper to Jenny. "Here. If you ever need to talk, this is my number."

To Dread or Not to Dread?

I intensely dislike the term *terrible twos*. The least of its inaccuracies is the word *twos*. It actually starts anywhere from fifteen to eighteen months and is usually over with by age two and a half. But the real pejorative is the word *terrible*. Certainly children exhibit negative behavior at this stage. Certainly the temper emerges about now, the obstinacy surfaces, the demands escalate. But that is not terrible. It is necessary and desirable, and very few parents fail to live through it. Unfortunately, when parents are impaired by alcohol or drugs or when extreme circumstances cut their patience short, the children suffer unduly and a tragic few die by the hands of the people who ostensibly love them.

This time of change and redirection is inevitable for each and every child. Most children will exhibit negative behavior. From about eighteen months on, three things happen in the child's life simultaneously. Each alone is unsettling. Coming together, they hit the toddler with a triple whammy that makes this short period of life the most tumultuous the child will experience until the early teens grab the kid by the throat.

You may think your patience is being tested. But believe me, the child has it worse.

1. Frustration

At eighteen months, Brian Jasper was ready to take on the world. He could walk steadily, run (sort of), and climb like nobody's business. The little plastic slide that he had found so exciting was unused now, too tame for him.

As skilled as his tiny body was, it was not nearly mature enough or coordinated enough to fulfill his dreams. He wanted to do far bigger, more ambitious things. Climb up on long-suffering Dum and ride him, for example. Run far and fast. Keep up with Daddy. Make his tricycle work. He was frustrated by his own clumsiness and lack of coordination.

At the same time, his inexperienced baby intellect could not always calculate in advance the consequences when his much-improved toddler body did things. He would try to stack blocks with rounded sides, not yet sophisticated enough to know that the sides have to be flat. Big things failed to fit into little receptacles. Canned goods rolled wrong. Toys refused to do what he wanted.

How did he take out his frustrations? Screaming and tantrums. It was like letting the cork blow on the champagne bottle. The pressure needed a release; the screaming was it. Marsha and Tom did not immediately see the frustration. They saw only the external behavior, and it appalled them.

2. Independence

Mr. Rogers, that gentle, saintly pied piper of public television, has been feeding you a line.

For years he sang to the kiddies, "Everything grows together," meaning that body parts grow proportionally as the child gets older. They don't. Proportions change, which is why a baby just past one doesn't look at all like a baby approaching two. But development varies in other ways as well.

Each major kind of development in a child follows its own independent time line. Sexual maturity, for example, proceeds at its own pace without regard to physical development or emotional development. In fact, emotional development usually lags, contributing to teens' angst and growing pains. This is the complex process by which a child achieves the ultimate independence of becoming wholly and completely his or her own person. Brian and Sara were just entering the beginning of it.

No matter when a child begins to crawl or walk or speak those first tentative words, *individuation* begins in earnest around fifteen months. Individuation is when the little ones get that first delicious taste of independence. That means the toddler no longer experiences the same thoughts, the same decisions, the same wants and desires, the same dislikes, or the same values as Mommy and Daddy. Although the toddler is woefully outclassed, he or she will make those brand new independent thoughts known.

Sara, for instance, wanted the decorative wooden salad bowl on the dining-room table. Grandma didn't want her to have it. Sara insisted, climbing up on a chair to reach for it. Frustrated, Grandma put it on top of the refrigerator and pulled Sara off the chair and set her on the floor.

Six months ago it would have been sufficient to tell Sara she could not have the bowl. No longer. The new, independent Sara would not take no for an answer. Also, her tenacity and attention span had matured and improved to the point that she could remember where the bowl had gone and that she wanted it. Five minutes later, Grandma found Sara on the kitchen counter, still climbing, headed for the top of the refrigerator.

Grandma saw Sara's persistence as an instance of being naughty. Somewhere deep within, below conscious level, Sara probably regarded it as a necessary statement of her new separateness from Grandma and everyone else.

3. Dependence

Brian Jasper, at age fifteen months, woke up one morning to realize it is one big scary world out there. He was doing things he never did before, achieving little victories that had previously eluded him, seeing things with new and more mature eyes. For instance, the big dog down the street that once had seemed like a modified version of Dum suddenly revealed itself as a totally separate menace, not in the least like Dum.

Below conscious level Brian realized he was in over his head. Just as he was beginning, like Sara, to exercise his independence, he felt a greater need to cling, to hold on to his source of security, Mommy and Daddy. This balancing act, this pull from two directions, would bring immense emotional and social turmoil to his next year or two.

Mommy and Daddy would see only the surface, the acting out that this cosmic tussle generated, and call it the terrible twos. They would not grasp that down inside Brian (and Sara and every other one- to two-year-old) a phenomenal struggle was taking place. These children would pry their own unique identities out from their families', forging a brand new self, a *Me* that had never existed before.

Terrible twos? Wonderful twos! For it is here an individual child is truly born.

2. CROSSING THE GREAT DIVIDE

SEPARATION AND INDIVIDUATION

The way of salvation cannot lie
in melting people down into a mass,
but on the contrary in their
separation and individuation.

THEODOR HAECKER

Eighteen-month-old Brian Jasper carried his Dr. Seuss book over to Daddy, tossed the book up into Daddy's lap, then followed it, clambering up. But Daddy was not allowed to hold the book. Brian held the book and turned the pages when he pleased.

In another home, eighteen-month-old Sara Lawton threw her first real tantrum. It wasn't bad for a first attempt.

Both of these children were defying authority to some degree and taking their destiny into their own hands. By manipulating his book himself, Brian was taking control in a very mild way. Though largely symbolic, that almost-unnoticed act was highly significant.

Sara's tantrum? Very obvious. There are people who would call her actions disobedience, even sin, because children, said Paul in Ephesians, are to obey their parents. I'll not argue the theology. I will point out, however, that defiance is absolutely necessary for growth. Through it, the child establishes an identity apart from his or her parents.

Both of these toddlers, then, were becoming individuals. And it wasn't easy for either of them.

Splitting Between
Good and Bad

There is a watershed in this process of individuation, what you might call the first of several continental divides. Up until about eighteen months, things go one way. After that, they go another. The parent need not particularly assist a child in successfully mastering the lessons of this unique time, but parents can unwittingly prevent or alter the necessary lessons. The child may then bump into problems later as he or she grows and matures.

One of the lessons of this short window of opportunity is that the world is not entirely black and white, good and bad.

When Sara was fifteen months old, she loved to snuggle in Mommy's lap as Jenny read to her. Jenny fed her, played with her in her bath, took her out for walks. Sara felt loved and saw her mommy as all good. Hours later, Jenny refused to let Sara play in cold mud puddles when they went for a walk. Exceedingly angry with Mommy, Sara felt unloved and was certain Mommy was a bad person. Well, Sara didn't love Mommy either. So there!

To a toddler, the world and all who are in it are black or white—no shades of gray here. Mommy or any other primary caretaker is all good or all bad. In a strange, symbolic sense, life is literally split into two different mutually exclusive conditions.

Comes the watershed of eighteen months, and the two distinct Mommies—the good person and the bad person—integrate into one person capable of different responses. It's the giant first step down that long, long road to a secure personal identity. The child comes to understand that another person has an identity *separate* from himself or herself and that that identity is *complex*. The only way this occurs successfully is if the toddler experiences what we call *narcissistic wounding*.

Providing Narcissistic-Wounding Experiences

The Narcissus of Greek fable was a handsome youth who fell in love with his own reflection in a limpid pool. He suffered the first and most severe narcissistic wounding—he either fell in and drowned or wasted away to death, depending on the version. At any rate, the flower we call narcissus sprang up where he died.

Narcissism is love of self, or self-centrism. In the beginning, baby's survival and development depend totally upon his or her every single need being met by others. An infant, more so than any other human being, truly is the center of the universe, and that is certainly as it should be.

But life being what it is, that sort of self-centrism cannot go on forever. Narcissistic wounding is the term used for the stabbing realization that the child is not the center of the universe after all. The world was not created to cater to the child's every desire. Life, to quote the philosopher, is inherently unfair.

When the child at age twelve months or so first discovers the nasty reality of life, Mommy—or whoever it was who denied his or her request, whatever it was—is a bad person. There's that dichotomy of black and white. What Mommy did wasn't good. As that watershed age arrives, the child grasps the *reason* for not getting what he or she wants—Mommy or another caregiver wants something different, and Mommy is a separate individual with an inde pendent agenda.

All this occurs down below a rational, conscious, ver bal level. And a lesson taught so deep stays forever. Lessons on the bottom of the pile of life's wisdom last longest. So does the blank space, the non-lesson, if for some reason the lesson is not adequately taught.

What goes wrong if narcissistic wounding and its com panion lesson, integration of "good" and "bad," never take root? Relationships suffer.

1. *Relationships with Others Suffer.* Interpersonal relation ships almost never succeed if these lessons are not learned.

Even at eighteen months, little Sara had a strongly assertive personality. She knew what she wanted, and she knew that she wanted it. She was also rapidly learning that when Mommy had to study for her chemistry final, Sara's desires ended up on the back burner, if they were on the stove at all. As painful as it was for Mommy to delay Sara's gratifications, it taught an important truth: Sara was not the linchpin of existence.

Sara also learned that she and Grandma had something in common: Grandma knew what *she* wanted and knew that she wanted it also. In fact, little Sara and matronly Grandma seemed constantly at loggerheads. It was a con trol thing, a power thing, a personality thing. *My will versus your will; let's see who wins.* Irritating as it may be, it happens very frequently between babies and their primary adults. Through this interplay, as abrasive and upsetting as it might be (particularly to Grandma), Sara learned another useful lesson: It is not someone else's job to gratify her every whim. Sara must make her own way at times.

In contrast, I'm thinking of a woman named Ruth and her two daughters, Susan, fourteen, and Sherry, seventeen. Emotionally detached, Ruth's husband, Rick, did not get involved with the girls' upbringing significantly, which is to say that during their watershed years, he was not a major participant. Ruth and Rick eventually divorced.

Now, Ruth had experienced a great deal of neglect and unnecessary sacrifice in her own childhood. Anxious that her girls enjoy the pampered childhood she herself had been denied, she catered to them from the very beginning. The lesson Susan and Sherry learned during their watershed years was, "Someone owes it to you. Yell loud, and you'll get it."

In the jargon of the counseling trade, they were *entitled*. They figured, in other words, that they were entitled to receive what they wanted. The good old-fashioned term is *spoiled rotten*. The basis of that spoilage is a failure to experience the narcissistic wounding necessary for good emotional health, and it happened in their case at eighteen months.

What is the prognosis for Sherry and Susan? For one thing, entitled children are highly volatile. Another word for this is *labile*. That is, they experience severe mood swings. Susan typifies that, one moment smothering her mom with love and attention and the next, bitterly rejecting her.

"Yeah," worldly-wise Sherry agreed. "She can be sickening sweet, especially when she wants something or she just got something, and the next thing you know, she's yelling and screaming when she doesn't get what she wants. And not just at Mother, either. At school too."

If you've been analyzing this behavior, you've noticed that it is much like the toddler's concept of the all-good, all-bad Mommy. Exactly so. Susan never learned that primal lesson in integration, and its ghost haunted her thirteen years later.

With this black-white dichotomy, can Susan establish any kind of lasting relationship? Not well, no. Most people will find her terribly hard to live with; anyone else with her problem would find her absolutely impossible. She will also have difficulty maintaining employment, inevitably drifting from job to job and calling all her previous bosses unprintable names.

And what of Sherry? She didn't seem as volatile as her sister. Susan's battles turned outward; Sherry's turned in.

2. The Relationship with Oneself Suffers. During her watershed year Sherry missed the message that she, too, is neither all good nor all bad. For Sherry, the dichotomy was not so much toward the outside world, though that also played a part in her problems, but toward Sherry, herself. Part of a necessary lesson growing up is learning that both good and bad are also integrated within ourselves.

A toddler doesn't recognize any bad side. The toddler is right. Always. In Ruth's case she rarely, if ever, showed her girls any side of themselves that was less than perfect and forever right, the side that has to set firm internal limits and enforce self-discipline.

Punished for violating school rules and occasionally

state and county ordinances, Sherry blamed the system, the officials, the stupid nonsensical rules, the weather . . . You've met that kind before. It was never Sherry's fault.

Not once in her life had Sherry ever said, "It's my fault. I'm sorry." Forgiveness, the foundation of Christ's work, totally escaped her.

Sherry and Susan were, so to speak, not as bad as they could be. There is a step beyond entitlement, *exemption*. This person believes, *I am exempt from the laws of man and nature. I am above all that. Laws are to keep others in line. I'm so smart I don't need laws; they're not for me* . . .

Can you go overboard with attempts at narcissistic wounding? Absolutely. Pause to ponder the pattern here. Through that first year, a baby's every whim ought to be served. This is how the tiniest child learns trust. *I am provided for; I now know that I can trust others to provide what I require.* Ultimately that message will grow into, *I can trust my heavenly Father to provide every need.*

Now the parents must ease off pampering and reverse themselves; the toddler's priorities must be interwoven into other people's priorities. The child no longer always comes first. This is just as important as the initial pampering to instill the new lesson: *I can trust fully, even though I am not at the center of the universe.* Because of the nature of the child's windows of opportunity, the lessons cannot be reversed; you cannot prioritize first and pamper second.

Beware, too, the danger of instilling a "worm theology." The "worm" comes from the line in Scripture that says, in effect, "I am less than nothing. I am a worm and not a man" (see Ps. 22:6). Worm theologians have absolutely nothing positive to say about themselves or anyone else. Worm theologians are not worthy of any good thing. Children who are constantly put down and thrust aside will develop that outlook very early. If so, it will color their view of themselves and others their whole lives.

Ruth, always and ever ranked in second place (or lower) by her busy parents, developed just such an outlook. To combat it she went overboard in the opposite direction. The effects of the neglect she experienced extended into her daughters, and if Sherry and Susan bore children of their own, it would surely stretch its cold fingers into the third generation.

Ample opportunity to impart these important lessons, fortunately (or perhaps unfortunately, parents might say), is provided by the toddler himself or herself. It is just at this age that the child earnestly develops a mind of his or her own and the assertiveness to insist upon it.

Handling the Toddler's Negativism Positively

Who am I, and what are my limits?

Little Brian Jasper defined himself by taking over some of the milder prerogatives that had been his parents'—holding his own book while being read to, feeding himself, dressing himself (he made a mess of it, totally incapable of handling the task, but that didn't keep him from his favorite cry, "*I* do it! *I do it!*").

Baby Sara defined herself by opposing anything Grandma wanted. She showed that her will was different and separate by contrasting it with Grandma's, and to a lesser extent, Mommy's. The constant negativeness and opposition drove dear Grandma right out of her tree.

How do adults help these struggling new individuals? How do you keep a positive relationship with a child who screams and opposes? There is much the Jaspers and Lawtons can do. Each of these sets of parents would have to adjust and fine-tune the general suggestions given below to their specific circumstance. Brian, for example, is an easy baby; Sara is not. An older child, twelve and up, has a strong ability to reason and to understand abstracts. These little ones do not.

1. Consistency

Consistency is drawing a line, an obvious line, so that the child can test it and thereby define his or her own limits. Children find the walls of their own uniqueness by bouncing off them. That line is always drawn, need I mention, in the best interests of the child. Not expediency. Not convenience. Not the parents' whims or quirks, but in the best interests of the child.

Consistency is not changing "no" one day to "yes" the next simply because it's convenient to do so or inconvenient to maintain the rule. Put out the effort to maintain a uniform rule of the house.

Consistency is not extending and then withholding privilege. A child allowed to do something one day should be permitted to do it the next. There are exceptions, of course, as when a parent discovers that some activity, previously allowed, is actually dangerous.

"I let Brian play with the alphabet blocks I had when I was a baby," Marsha said one day. "They were my mother's when she was a baby; they really are very old and battered. Then I discovered the paint on them is lead-based. Brian was really torqued when I took them away from him."

Curiously, consistency is also change. As children grow in size, awareness, and personality, a parent, in order to be consistent, must change tactics with that growth. To a toddler, "Do it" is sufficient. A grade-schooler ought to have an explanation; it's a learning tool. A high-schooler should have the conscience, self-discipline, and wisdom to know why without much explanation. To acknowledge and work with the child's changing capabilities is consistency.

It seems at times that consistency adds to friction. Would it not be better to just give in? No. Keeping the line clearly drawn minimizes friction in the long run and teaches the vital precept that there are indeed lines. God Himself laid down important lines, which we cross to our woe. This simple lesson of toddlerhood offers cosmic ramifications.

2. The Primary Caregiver

"I don't get it," Jenny said, really miffed. "I'm more flexible with Sara, I play with her, and we don't butt heads nearly as much. But Sara still prefers Mom to me. She can't get along with Mom, but she goes to her every time anyway."

Remember the toddler's frustrating tussle between dependence and independence? A part of the dependence is an extreme attachment to the primary caregiver (sometimes, from the caregiver's point of view, too much so).

The toddler periodically checks on the caregiver's where-abouts, making certain he or she is near.

"Of course I'm near," Sara's grandma sniffed. "I'm always near, until Jenny gets home. Why should Sara cling so? And yet, when I try to cuddle her, she squirms to get down."

Marsha Jasper, a stay-at-home mom, has exactly the same complaint. "It's not like I'm away for long periods. And Brian wants me but he doesn't want me. He'll come to me and push me away! I don't get it."

Toddlers at this age possess three main interests: relating to their primary caregiver (the dependence part), exploring the world around them (the independence part), and mastering physical motor skills.

An effective caregiver makes sure there are ample opportunities for a balance of all three interests throughout the toddler's day. This means it sometimes won't be in the best interest of the child to sit and cuddle, even though that's what you most want to do. It might serve the child better for you to play together rather than to just hold him or her. Just as children's needs change in the arena of need gratification, so do they change in this area of cuddling and holding.

3. Separation

Marsha and Tom Jasper knew better than to put Brian in the nursery during church services. Most children cry a couple minutes and lose themselves in play. Not Brian. "He was still screaming ten minutes after I left him," Marsha said, describing the first Sunday she took advantage of the nursery. "I went back to check on him and assured him it was okay and that he could trust the nice ladies in the nursery. Twenty minutes later he was still screaming. So I took him out, for the sake of the nursery people. We tried one other time with the same results; so now Brian stays with us. It's just easier."

What does Brian do in church? Actually, he's a good baby, sitting on a lap, turning pages in the hymnal, reading one of the books Marsha brings along from home. He's not a problem. The problem lies elsewhere.

An important step in the separation and individuation process is called *object constancy*. The theory: An object, in this case the caregiver, is constant about returning from an absence. Having that caregiver around all the time is called *object permanence*. The object is permanently at hand.

Lessons in object constancy should begin before the child reaches a year of age. They will still "take" during this second year, but they will be more difficult.

Sara learned object constancy very early as her mommy went off to school in the morning and Grandma stepped out of the picture when Mommy got home in the afternoon. The caregiver left. The caregiver will return. Every time.

Because Brian's primary caregiver rarely left him, Brian had never learned the lesson well. Now, during his second year, was the time to teach it. Waiting until later would make it all the harder for him and his parents both.

How do you teach object constancy? Mini-separations. Much reassurance. Prompt returns. Here's a possible scenario:

MARSHA: Brian, Mrs. Schwartz from next door is going to watch you a few minutes while I run to the store. I will be back soon.

BRIAN: Waaa!

MARSHA: She's a very nice lady, and she'll take good care of you. I will come back soon.

BRIAN: Waaa!

EXIT MARSHA.

Marsha returns later, as promised. She makes over Brian, hugging him with much laughter and reassurance.

When she leaves, Brian is totally bent out of shape and may well make Marsha painfully aware that he is unhappy with her. But the lesson has been offered, and below conscious, articulate level, Brian has received it.

After several such mini-separations, Marsha and Tom stretch out the time. On every occasion, they reassure Brian that they will return soon. *I will return. I will return.* Emphasize it.

Within a few months, Marsha should leave Brian at the church nursery regardless of whether he screams. Bribes are not out of the question. (However, Marsha should *not* leave bribes such as cookies for use during her absence unless she provides cookies for all the children. It's not nice to treat Brian while the others go without.) Treats are best and most effective when used following the separation. How ought Marsha present a treat?

Not: "Here's a treat for being a good boy." He may not have been, and anyway, treats (roughly equated with love in a child's eyes) should not be contingent upon behavior.

Better: "Here's a treat. I really missed you, and I'm

glad to be with you again." No conditions, no limits. Just love. For a child, remember, relationships are everything.

As much as Marsha complained about her son's excessive attachment, it served her below conscious level by making her feel needed. She was the only sun in someone's sky. Before she could handle the separations well, she would have to self-talk herself into accepting the truth that it was in Brian's best interest to do this.

Periodically leaving a toddler in the care of competent caregivers is also another occasion of narcissistic wounding. This separation certainly isn't the toddler's idea. And yet, the outcome is satisfactory. Combined, object constancy plus narcissistic wounding teaches that the world may not rotate around the child, but the world will come around again.

4. Contests of Wills

Sara sat in her high chair in a complete grump, lower lip thrust out, arms folded. Grandma sat beside the high chair in a complete grump, lips tight and grim, arms folded. Sara would not drink her milk. Grandma would not budge on the issue.

Grandma knows, because Jenny informed her, that this test of wills comes from Sara's groping for a separate identity. But Grandma also knows that she knows best about Sara's welfare. She isn't gonna give in.

The rest of us have probably experienced parallels to Sara's situation. Are you in a dead-end job that is not rewarding, where you have no say in what happens and no suggestion you make is ever taken seriously? Stultifying. That's what it's like to a child who never, ever gets to win a contest of wills. To a toddler just beginning to explore his or her individuality, it's even more discouraging.

I do not advocate caving in in the face of undesirable behavior; nor do I advocate extreme leniency. There are other lessons to be learned. But giving a child choices teaches great lessons also. The toddler learns, *I am an individual. My desires count.* That can be supported verbally ("Good choice, Brian!" "Okay, Sara, if you wish. Let's do it your way.") but it cannot be taught by rational preaching. To learn, the child must make a decision that is honored by others.

Certainly Grandma can be judicious in this. She wouldn't let Sara run out into the street simply because Sara thinks it's a good idea. But if Sara doesn't want her milk now, offer it later.

In the Jaspers' home, Brian wants *Good Dog, Karl* to be read to him for the 400th time although Marsha recently bought him three wonderful new books. So Marsha reads *Good Dog, Karl* for the 401st time. Then she might read one of the new ones as well.

Meeting children's contests of will is the same as international negotiations or marital give-and-take. Sometimes the parents win, sometimes the child's will is honored, sometimes it's a compromise, and sometimes it's a matter of both desires being met, as with Marsha's compromise about which books to read.

Manipulating contests of wills to assure some victories for the child minimizes the possibility of tantrums. Although I don't suggest walking on eggs for fear of tantrums, it's a nice fringe benefit.

5. Dealing with Tantrums

A temper tantrum at this age is usually like a cork popping. Overwhelmed by frustrations or emotions that the toddler can neither understand nor control, the kid goes ballistic. Emotion generates a lot of energy. Watch rabid fans at a sports event or the announcement of the new Miss America. All that yelling, the tears and laughter, are means of dissipating the energy of emotion.

Some kids can dissipate that energy physically, which is to say that not all children throw tantrums. Personality figures strongly in this also. Some children are naturally shy or carefree to the extent that they can blow off frustration and anger harmlessly.

Brian, for example, would throw what one might call a tantrum, but he wasn't trying to get his own way. His inability to perform some feat or master some little skill—like getting into his sweat pants himself or making a stack of blocks stay stacked—might touch off an episode of stomping and screaming. Such episodes occurred primarily during play, or attempted play, and almost never in public.

Although she didn't catch on at first, eventually Marsha rightly interpreted the sessions as explosive outpourings of emotional energy, and she treated them as such. She soothed, she hugged, she purred, she calmed, and then she helped. Whatever the frustrating goal was, if possible she aided him in achieving it.

Then there was Sara.

As usual, Grandma knew what was best. She wanted to tie a big bib around Sara before the chocolate ice cream was served. Sara wanted none of that. She had formed an attachment to her much-smaller Big Bird bib (actually a drool bib).

Grandma protested that it was too small to protect Sara's pretty dress. (Did I mention that all this was happening in the food court of a large shopping mall? Such displays almost always take place in prominent places where the world is watching.) Grandma tried a compromise—Big Bird underneath and the big bib on top. No. How about Big Bird on top and the full-size bib underneath? No.

Frustrated, Grandma enforced her authority and put the big bib on Sara anyway. And that's when the tantrum erupted.

Grandma was now in this too deep to back out, and besides, she'd never allowed tantrums in Jenny. She gave Sara a swat. The tantrum intensified. She glanced around guiltily at the extensive audience. Furious, she scooped up the thrashing, flailing child and marched out the door. Sara's little black patent leather shoes left bruise marks on Grandma's thighs that didn't fade for three weeks.

The child who goes out of control, in a way, is asking for help to get back under control. This is an energy overflow, not a garden of delights. In the beginning, the child doesn't really want to do this. The parents may be angry or frightened by the outburst, but the child is angrier and more frightened. The child doesn't understand what is happening and has no way of imagining that someday this can be controlled. Only later, if the child learns that a tantrum will achieve the desired effect of garnering attention or a wanted end, will the tantrum become voluntary.

A first step in dealing with a blowup is simply to let the child throw the fit in safety and give the clear message every time: *I don't care to be in your presence while you're acting this way.*

That means you don't give *any* attention (positive or negative) to your toddler during the course of the blowup. Keep in mind that in a small child's eyes, negative attention is better than no attention at all. At home, the child simply is sequestered in a safe room until the explosion subsides.

When Grandma put Sara in her room during a tantrum, Sara refused to stay there. The tantrum intensified. There's that dependence-independence dichotomy again. In response, Grandma could use an elastic cord to keep the door slightly ajar. Then she would be present but not present, and she could still hear and monitor Sara for matters of safety.

Out in public, retreating to the vehicle, the curb, or a rest room is the best bet. When the storm subsides, take up life again. Screaming and yelling, spanking, threatening, hitting—responses of that sort teach nothing and do very little to curb the tantrum or the prospect of a repeat performance.

Responding to a temper tantrum by ignoring it also helps a child experience a valuable lesson in splitting—indeed, two lessons. The child sees in the most frightening and violent terms the side of himself or herself that is not very pretty. You bet a full-blown tantrum scares the child who is throwing it. And yet, look! The caregiver does not reject (in the child's eyes, cease loving) the kid despite that nasty side. Then, of course, there is the lesson that attention or any other desired thing is not forthcoming as a result of the tantrum.

I am not always nice, but I am always loved. What a crucial message.

6. Reinforcement of Love

When the tantrum has subsided into tears and wailing it is time to pick up, to cuddle, to reassure. *I love you.* Not *I love you anyway* or *I love you now that that's over and out of the way.* Nothing conditional. Just, *I love you.* You say it, not only with words, but also with a kiss, a hug, a smile.

Even when you don't gratify the child's desire instantly, you still love him or her unconditionally. Even when the kid is the most obstinate, obnoxious, frustrating being on earth, you still love him or her unconditionally. Over and over, you set the stage for an abiding understanding of unconditional love. Again, there are cosmic consequences: God loves unconditionally, but until your child has experienced that kind of love here in life, he or she cannot grasp it.

In these negative situations, and also in every positive one, the caregiver is the key to a successful outcome (by that I mean an outcome that teaches the child something wholesome and useful). During the plethora of situations a day thrusts upon child and caregiver alike, the adult adopts a number of roles the child needs.

The Caregiver's Roles

A primary caregiver takes on two major roles at this point in a child's life. The first, which every parent assumes, is that of the authoritarian; the second is the role of consultant.

The Authoritarian

Many fathers have this role down pat. Many mothers need a lot of work in this area. ("Wait until your father gets home" is not a position of authority.) Of course the opposite is often true, as well; mothers can be authoritarians just as easily as fathers. Children in these families know there is a boss, and they know it isn't them. The authority figure, then, does two things:

1. Sets the Rules. A toddler must know what is right and unacceptable. Small children are dichotomous. Their sense of black and white extends far beyond personality assessment into every phase of life. Children are born with a sense of absolute ethics. To a child, a thing is never good on one occasion but bad on another. It's either good or it isn't.

The authority figure determines what is good and what is not. Always. What is good, I repeat, is that which best serves the child's interests. This may well be the opposite of what the child thinks are his or her best interests. I do not suggest bending to a child's wants and desires continually. Serving the child's long-range interests is the goal.

2. Takes the Role of Authority Away from the Children. Rephrased, taking authority means making it clear to the child that he or she need not assume the role of adult. This knowledge comes as an immense relief to a toddler— below the verbal level, of course. It is comforting to know it's safe to be a child.

This is an immensely important part of an adult's duty. A child, and particularly a toddler, is not capable of handling adult responsibility. When circumstances force the child to assume an adult role, and that does happen, the child falls under immense pressure. *What if something goes wrong? What if a choice is the wrong one?* A child can be scarred for life by making a wrong decision he or she was never prepared to make in the first place. Children have no wisdom, no background, to be adults with adult choices; that's the whole idea of childhood.

At this age, no one is going to ask the child to baby-sit or stay home alone. (Well, all right. Some recent news stories reveal that such ugliness does sometimes occur. I'm talking about you. You will not.) Later, this part of the role of authority figure will become more immediate.

When a child of ten is assigned baby-sitting duties, for instance, even on a limited basis, that child will probably suffer nothing more than aggravation because the little ones will not listen or obey. Mom is gone only ten or fifteen minutes. But in that brief quarter hour, little children can get into a whole lot of trouble. Ninety-nine times out of a hundred, the fifteen minutes will pass safely. That hundredth time, perhaps, the fire department will arrive at the door before Mom does. And will the ten-year-old feel responsible for the accident or tragedy? Yes. His or her whole life long.

A child of two should *never* be in the driver's seat. Certainly, let the child make some decisions and then live by them. But never permit the toddler to set rules or influence major decisions. As much as the toddler, and later the child, claims to want to take on these roles, real comfort comes in not having to. *I don't have to be a grown-up. I am free to be a kid.*

A more diffuse role than authoritarian, and one that is harder to define, is that of consultant.

The Consultant

The consultant assists. When the child needs help, the consultant is there. But more important—and this is the delicate part—the consultant does not do *for* the child; the consultant helps the child do.

Helps Solve Problems. I think this was my favorite role as a daddy. Now, my son, Matthew, solves most of his problems himself. But when he was small, my ego absolutely glowed when he needed his daddy to help out.

Broken toy? Mommy fix. Can't make this toy work? Daddy help.

More than once, however, I frustrated Matthew with my help. On one occasion I remember vividly, Matthew needed help getting all his books into a bag. He was becoming frustrated, even angry, because his attempts weren't succeeding.

Good old Daddy to the rescue. In my vanity I shuffled the books, arranged them by size, and they slid in. "There. See?"

Matthew wailed, "I didn't want you to do it. I wanted you to show me how to do it."

Matthew had the clearer vision, better by far, of what a problem solver ought to be.

As you solve your toddler's problems and make wrong things right again to the best of your ability, don't forget to include the child in the solution.

Grants Wishes. Here is another aspect of the consultant role that strokes a parent's ego. Your child makes a wish. You grant it. Who was the most powerful person in *Cinder-*

ella? The fairy godmother. The parent is called upon to play that powerful fairy-godmother part, if only on small occasions. A bit of the fairy godmother lies within us all.

Do you grant your child's every wish? Of course not. And after I've said *of course not* you will point out that Ruth, the distraught mother of Sherry and Susan, had granted nearly every one of her daughters' desires. Yes, some parents do go overboard, usually in response to unfinished agendas within their own psyche. They do so to their children's detriment. That was the situation Ruth found herself in.

Validates. Parents rarely see this as an important part to play, and there is not the same surge of ego-stroking that problem solvers and wish granters enjoy. The child, though, requires validation as much as any other gift a parent can bestow.

A parent validates a child in several ways. Simply acknowledging the child and paying attention is one of the easiest and most common. "Look, Mommy!" should never go unanswered.

Even the negative response, "I can't look now, honey; I'm driving in heavy traffic," validates the child's request. The child was noticed and responded to, even if the response was not the best possible. The child is an individual. The child matters.

A parent also validates a child by accepting the child's decisions, even in trivial matters. Remember that what is trivial to a parent is probably very important to the child at that moment. It may not matter to the child later; it may not have mattered a minute ago. If it matters now, it matters. When Sara threw her tantrum over a bib, the business mattered to her at that point simply because it mattered!

Shall I have grape jelly or strawberry jam this morning? Many adults are not awake enough at breakfast to make a decision, or even to care. In contrast, when the child decides, it's momentous.

"Good choice, kid!"

That's validation.

The bottom line of this role fulfillment extends into eternity. In a real sense, to the toddler, Mommy and Daddy are God. Mommy and Daddy can do anything. It is from Mommy and Daddy, especially Daddy, that children will develop a concept of who God is and how much their Father in heaven loves them. How many of us as practicing Christians bring our laundry list of problems to God and ask Him to solve them for us? And we bring along wish lists, too, asking God in prayer to grant them, ticking off the items. How much do we seek His validation for our choices and our lives? That's the power of the parent in the toddler's life.

Promoting Your Child's First Attempts at Independence

As separation and individuation proceed, however clumsily or fraught with friction, another aspect of maturation grows simultaneously—independence. Separation and independence go hand in hand, and as parents promote the one they are, in essence, promoting the other as well. There are, however, a number of good things parents can do to help the child through this first phase of separation.

One of the best is simply to understand the monumental tussle going on inside that little human being. Another is to allow the child to make mistakes. Incidentally, this is true whether the child be a Brian or Sara, or a fifteen-year-old.

Helping Your Child Experiment with Independence and Dependence

They were going to be late for church, and Marsha was frustrated. "Brian, for Pete's sake, sit still! I can't get your shoes on when you're wiggling like this."

"I do it!"

"Not this time. We're late. You can do it some other time."

"*I* do it!"

"They have to be on the right feet. Now sit still!"

How often does a variation on the above scenario play out in the lives of parents of one-plus-year-olds? The late hour added a sense of urgency to Marsha's situation there, but the mood of the moment happened over and over. Brian was too little to perform many of the tasks and functions he assigned himself, and Marsha's patience disintegrated as Brian fumbled around.

And therein lies a trap. It's far too easy, not to mention faster, for Marsha or Tom to do whatever needs be done than to let Brian try to do it. This serves the short-term goal, such as making it to church on time, but it works against the long-term goal of helping the child grow.

Childhood is a grand experiment to discover what works and what doesn't. How often have you thought,

"If I only knew then what I know now." So does a six-year-old. Experiment teaches through trial and error. Even a toddler must be given the opportunities to make mistakes.

Mistakes Help Growth

Thomas Edison, arguably the modern world's most fruitful inventor, would literally try hundreds of ideas before he hit upon the one that worked. One interviewer asked about that practice, commenting on the wastefulness of such a procedure. Mr. Edison pointed out that now he knew ninety-nine things that did not work. He's the one, you know, who claimed, "Genius is 1 percent inspiration and 99 percent perspiration."

Children learn as much, or more, from the things that do not work as they learn from things that do. Brian would try forcing a block into the heater grate. It wouldn't fit. He learned something then about matter and space. Remember that toddlers do not know what we think they should automatically know. They must learn about the world, and learning hands-on, so long as hands-on is safe, is the best teacher.

Brian got his shoes on the wrong feet 50 percent of the time. Actually, a little more than 50 percent. Once he had them on, he would mash down the Velcro flaps, sometimes closing the shoes snugly and sometimes not. He really didn't care whether his shoes fit right. Marsha did. This brings up another question. How do you correct the child's inadequacies and mistakes?

Marsha might say, "Here. They're on the wrong feet.

Let's switch them." Or, "They're too loose, Brian. Let me tighten the flaps."

On the other hand, she might say. "Good job! That looks like fun. Let me try it too." And she proceeds to take the shoes off and put them on the correct feet. A negative, fault-finding statement versus a positive statement. You're not going to score 100 percent on this. But may I suggest that whenever possible, whenever you can think of it, try for a positive statement. Build up. Praise.

There are other reasons we stymie our children's attempts at independence. The biggest one is fear.

Fear lurks in two different rooms of our hearts. One is fear for our children's safety. This is a justifiable fear, considering the recklessness of most toddlers. I do not advocate under-protection, but I certainly warn you to be on the lookout for overprotection.

There goes Brian, climbing up on Daddy's recliner. Might he fall? Quite possibly. So you evaluate the potential of the situation. Is he likely to hurt himself in a fall? Probably not. Carpeted floor, short drop. Then let him go, with supervision. He scrambles up into it, sits a moment, and squirms off, feetfirst. He and his body have just learned another mini-lesson about textures, distance, and his own capabilities.

The other fear is not so easy to spot—fear that your child will grow up.

"That's ridiculous!" Marsha huffed. "I *want* him to grow up."

As do we all, at least consciously. You will remember that Brian had a problem with object permanence because Marsha never left him. That's a sign that perhaps, deep,

deep down, she wanted him to stay little and cute and dependent.

Over-protectiveness is another sign of this underlying fear. So is a reluctance to encourage the child to do more mature things, such as feed himself or herself.

People do not see this fear in themselves. Countering it means the parents must each assay the other and believe what the other sees. It isn't easy.

This growing up, then, is not just painful for the kids. It's painful for the parents, too. It's rather like bicycling through life without training wheels.

Remember when you learned to ride a bike?

"I remember Daddy bolting on the training wheels, and off I went," Marsha recalled.

Jenny Lawton grinned. "Yeah. It was a Sunday afternoon after church. The bike was a birthday present. Dad held the seat and ran along beside, and down the street we went. Down the sidewalk, I mean. Wobble wobble! He's a strong man and I wore him out. It was one of the neatest days of my life."

"I remember learning about going down hills on one of my first times out," Tom answered. He grinned. "The hard way."

"My parents didn't teach me." Ruth, whose parents were wrapped up in church work, didn't smile. "It was a used bike one of the congregation members gave me. I got on it. Fell off. Got on. Fell off. Finally I could get it started rolling far enough to pedal. It was a long process." The smile arrived. "But I did it."

Guiding your child through this turbulent year is much like teaching the tot to ride a bike. First you hold on to the bike, all the while reassuring the child as you breathe heavily from the unaccustomed exertion of running alongside; then you have to let go. When the child falls, you kiss the boo-boo and start the whole process again. Over and over.

It helps, as you're doing this, that you in your adult wisdom understand the way bikes work and the way the laws of God and nature work. You know what is needed to master this skill. However, teaching your toddler how to build relationships, both with the self and also with others, is infinitely more difficult. There are no clear-cut rules that work for everyone, few clear timetables, no uniform circumstances. It's all a complex process involving an integrated set of socialization skills. In the next chapter, we'll look at some of them.

3. LEARNING LITTLE LESSONS OF LIFE

SOCIAL DEVELOPMENT

Train up a child in the way he
should go,
And when he is old he will not
depart from it.

PROVERBS 22:6

*J*enny Lawton took Sara to the park one afternoon.

"Want to get on the teeter-totter?" she asked Sara.

Sara ran to the swings. "No, swing."

Jenny lifted her into the toddler swing and pushed her up into the air. Sara squealed with laughter.

Suddenly, Sara started kicking. "Down! Down!" she demanded.

Jenny sighed. She lifted the squirming Sara out of the swing and put her on the ground.

"Tee'er," Sara said, running toward the teeter-totter.

"Okay," Jenny said. She sat her on the end of the teeter-totter that was on the ground. "Hold on to this handle." She placed Sara's hands on the handle. "I'll go over to the other side and help you go high up in the air."

Jenny walked to the other side of the teeter-totter. She pushed down on the board and Sara went up about two feet in the air.

"Higher," Sara said.

"Okay, just a little, though. Hold on tight." Jenny

pushed down again. Then she let Sara down to the ground with a gentle bump.

Sara tried to push herself back up with her feet, but she couldn't raise the heavy board. Instantly frustrated, she jumped off the teeter-totter and ran back to the swing.

This was getting old in a hurry. Wearily, Jenny trudged over to the swings. When would Sara find some darling little playmate and leave Jenny in peace?

Not for quite a while yet.

The Beginning of Socialization

I understand Jenny's frustration. Like butterflies in a rose garden, children flit from thing to thing, from idea to idea. Kids and adults have trouble relating for just that reason—short attention spans. Besides, that which appeals to the grown-up hardly ever piques the child's interest. The infantile behavior, the many messes, the indecision, and the irrational insistence all add their bits to a mystical and amazing bond between parent and child.

As a small child, our son, Matthew, was an exuberant eater. By this I don't mean that he wolfed down everything in sight. Rather, he cast his bread upon the waters . . . and upon the floor and upon anyone nearby and sometimes even upon the high-chair tray. He derived great pleasure from the food itself. Eating was secondary. Many is the time I cleaned up a mess under his high chair, wiping up peas and potatoes and jelly-side-down bread.

The very act of cleaning up after my son was an emotionally satisfying and invigorating thing for me. *Bonding* is the word. Consider how our heavenly Father must clean up messes we leave behind us as we go through life. Is the bonding as satisfying for Him as it is for me? I like to think so.

Infancy

When I was born, fathers were nuisances during birthing, pests to be shunted aside and harmlessly sequestered in cheerless waiting rooms stocked with outdated hunting and auto magazines. They were offered not a single shred of reading material on what a father should do. They were not allowed to see the birth, touch the baby, or interfere with hospital routine. Anyone who took a visible interest in the process was considered a wimp.

In today's prevailing opinion, a wimp is any man who resists taking an active part in the delivery. Traditionally, one of the father's roles is to introduce his child to the world. Perhaps that explains in part the immense emotional power new fathers experience when they are allowed to cut their child's umbilical cord. Symbolically and in fact, they are ushering their child from the mother out into the world.

The baby's first relationships, however, are not of the world. Mommy, and to a lesser extent, Daddy, are the only people in a newborn's life. That doesn't last long. Siblings and others are soon added to the child's repertoire of relationships. Still, Mommy and Daddy remain primary. Mommy is All Women. She is the foundation and point of reference from which the child will judge all female human beings later. Similarly, Daddy is All Men. Below conscious level, and sometimes consciously, the child will measure against Daddy every other man he or she ever meets.

Does a single-parent youngster thereby miss something important?

Yes.

One parent or two, the child's major socialization during the first year of life is his or her relationship with the primary caregiver. That relationship comes as the caregiver nurtures the child and attends to daily needs—feeding, changing diapers, cleaning up messes, cuddling, responding to the baby's cries. By the first birthday, if socialization has been successful thus far, the baby has learned to trust people by learning to trust the caregiver, presumably Mommy and Daddy. Here again, the parents serve as a model for the world at large. The stage is set for further socialization.

The Second Year

Mrs. Lennox had come to take care of Sara. Jenny's mom had recommended her. "An older lady, and no nonsense," Mom had described her. Jenny arrived home from work as eighteen-month-old Sara was eating her snack. All excited to see Mommy, Sara tipped over her glass of juice onto the floor.

"Sara!" snapped Mrs. Lennox. "That was a naughty girl. You need to be more careful!"

Jenny gaped. "Mrs. Lennox, she wasn't being naughty; she was being clumsy. She didn't mean to do it."

"She has to learn to be more careful."

Jenny let it pass. What else could she do? She handed

a washcloth to Sara and set her down on the floor. "Here. Can you show me how to wipe this up?"

Sara rubbed the washcloth all over the floor, merrily spreading juice.

"Jenny! What's the matter with you? She's just a baby. She can't clean this up. And look what she's doing to the floor!" Impatiently, Mrs. Lennox snatched the washrag out of Sara's hand and headed for the sink.

By now, you should be able to analyze the mechanics of that little exchange. Jenny had the right idea about giving Sara experiences with which to grow. Incidentally, note also Jenny's patience.

What were the lessons taught here?

"Nothing," you might respond. "It was just a momentary incident lasting less than a minute, a tiny blip in the day, not a life lesson."

Ah, but it was. The scores of little blips in a toddler's day, every single one of them, provide the real lessons, the teaching that sticks deepest. To us, annoying or scintillating blips are mere accretions to a lifetime of blips. Everything the toddler does and experiences, however, is new or nearly so. Everything teaches something. And at this age, a toddler blots up absolutely everything. Later, all those observations and experiences will form the foundation for everything else the child will do in life.

So again, what were the lessons in this blip of time?

1. Sara made a mistake. Actually, I don't really consider it a mistake although Sara, in her nonverbal wisdom, would. It was actually a spatial misjudgment; she didn't realize where her arm would be relative to the juice glass. Spilling her juice was certainly not a deliberate act.

2. *There is a consequence for each and every action.* The juice spilled. Whether intentional or not, the spill meant cleanup.

3. *People don't like me when I'm bad.* Mrs. Lennox admonished her, then walked away in anger.

4. *My attempt was a failure. I can't do it. I'm no good.* Is that really a message Sara received? It certainly was. Snatching away the washrag, scolding her, the anger, the verbal "She cannot do it" . . . all those actions registered. Don't think they didn't. It was one more datum in Sara's subconscious, one more message that would stick.

5. *Mommy loves me unconditionally.* Mommy didn't come unglued at the accident. Mommy kept her voice positive. After the accident, Mommy made physical contact—lifting Sara down, indicating favorable attention. Mommy continued to talk to Sara and include her in the situation.

Jenny's instincts as a parent were incredibly good. She understood without consciously thinking about it that a toddler who is punished or admonished for making a mistake will become a child afraid to try anything challenging. Failure hurts, and the pain feels unjust, which it is. Mrs. Lennox's outburst hurt Jenny as well and for the same reason—it was unjust.

Jenny did a great job of teaching the consequences lesson. She kept a cheerful, positive, upbeat attitude and let Sara help. Had Sara been able to complete her cleanup task, Jenny (or Grandma) could come along later and touch up what Sara missed—which would have been essentially all of the juice. But look at the excellent lesson Sara would have learned.

Sadly, negative lessons, such as in numbers 3 and 4, make a far greater impact than do positive ones. They stab deeper and last longer. I've seen an estimate that positive strokes should outnumber negative or critical strokes at least four to one for positive and negative to come anywhere near balancing out. I suspect four to one is low.

Two of the five lessons described previously were lessons in socialization—relationships with others—and a third, a lesson in self, greatly influences socialization. If a toddler learns from every supposedly inconsequential little moment, how can we, so to speak, make the most hay possible while the sun shines?

Making the Most of Each Lesson

Tom Jasper, who was into quantitative analysis anyway, decided one Saturday to keep track of the number of times in an hour that his eighteen-month-old Brian changed emotions. The change had to be from one strong, identifiable feeling to another. "Mildly bored," for example, didn't count separately if it ripened into "acutely bored." Bored would be bored. When he came up with eleven in one hour, he was sure he'd made a mistake and decided to count emotion shifts during another hour, half of which was spent at a playground. That time he got thirteen. These were quantum shifts from happy to sad, from angry to content, or whatever.

A "Far Side" cartoon by Gary Larson shows a theater

full of hummingbirds watching a nature film of human beings on a city street. The caption mentions that, of course, the film is greatly speeded up.

The smaller you are, the slower time goes compared with your own activities. Hummingbird hearts beat hundreds of times per minute. Elephants' typical heart rate is less than thirty. It's true of children also. Time speeds by ever faster as you age. To a small child, a day is a week long. The child whose attention span is measured in minutes does not feel the same rapid pace of plunging through changes of feelings as an adult would. This is another reason lessons such as Sara's spill make so telling an impression; the small child dwells longer upon each moment.

Remember, then, that the tyranny of time we adults face does not exist to the small child. A toddler always has enough time for whatever the day requires. The toddler will recognize the impatience in a parent's voice but not the concept of hurrying. To make the most of these blips in time, then, the first thought in these mini-lessons is to put time aside.

Dismiss Time Considerations

When Marsha was trying to get Brian's shoes on, when Sara was trying to clean up her juice mess, the lessons the mothers would forge had to be divorced from time.

For one thing, Mrs. Lennox should have backed off. Letting Sara help clean up her juice was worth the extra time it took.

Marsha might have carried Brian to the car without

his shoes on and said, "Brian, let's do this at church where we have more time." She would thereby have taught that time has importance without truncating Brian's shoe-donning experience, itself a little lesson.

Along with this knack for dismissing time, small children enjoy a singular freedom from goals. They love the process of doing something, as Brian did when he first climbed aboard his little plastic slide.

Enjoy the Process

A colleague, Dr. Brian Newman, recalls when he and his little daughter, Rachel, conducted an experiment to answer the question, "What is it like to be hit with a custard pie?" Vaudeville-comedy stuff. In the washable environs of the bathroom, they prepared pies and splooshed each other in the face.

"Okay, we had done it. Now I was ready to clean up and get on to something else," Brian recalled. "But Rachel sure didn't want to quit. She was still deep into the pleasure of conducting the experiment. The actual results were secondary."

Wisely, Brian allowed the moment to play out as long as Rachel wished. She thereby learned a wonderful lesson that could have come no other way. *I am important! Daddy spent time with our experiment and had as much fun as I did.* What a wonderful ego booster for a little girl. She and Brian both still talk about that happy occasion.

Happy occasion or sad, emotions are an immensely important part of a toddler's life, in part because they are so raw and intense.

Allow the Child to Show Emotions, Especially Being Upset

The following equation pertains:

$$\text{mental health} = \text{giving yourself permission}$$
$$\text{to experience a wide range of moods and behaviors}$$

Enjoying emotional health does not mean that your emotions are always so strongly controlled that you never give way to anger or remorse. Toddlers are as emotionally healthy and alive as a person ever gets, and toddlers let it all hang out. What you see is what the toddler feels that moment, and it will probably change in the next moment, as Tom Jasper learned to his amazement. How does a parent enhance the child's lessons at an emotional level?

For several reasons, a toddler requires the freedom to be upset. Being furious or dreadfully upset is frightening to a little child. *Will this uncontrollable emotion last forever? It hurts!* The child has no bank of past knowledge to know how to handle his or her emotions or even what they are. The child needs the parent's support with, "It's okay to be mad. Go for it! It's all right."

Only by experiencing their emotions can toddlers learn about them. That means literally living through them. "Don't cry. Be good. Stay calm," are damaging commands. Not only is the child too immature to follow such commands and control strong emotions (a lot of adults aren't mature enough either!), the command itself invalidates the feeling. Instead of the child's learning, "I feel intense emotions that will pass with time, and it's okay," the child learns, "Stifle it. Your emotions aren't worth feeling."

Also avoid sending the message that if the child gets angry, somehow Mommy and Daddy's approval will be lost.

I'm not suggesting that wild and hairy temper tantrums are the way to go, but displays of anger serve a valuable purpose. It takes many lessons, many little blips in a day, over a long period of time before the child can sort out the feelings that well up within. Sorting comes first. Controlling comes a slow second.

Letting anger and upset feelings run their course tells the child one more important message: *You are not perfect, but you are loved as you are.* Remember the splitting phenomenon? To integrate the nice with the not-so-nice, the child must be able to see the whole picture.

Help Your Toddler Learn
Responsibility and Consequences

Tom gave Brian a choice. "Do you want to go with me to the store, or do you want to go with Mommy to the Ferngolds' to pick up some borrowed books?" Brian loved grocery stores. He also loved to visit the Ferngolds, with their three (count 'em, three!) fluffy white bichon frise dogs. Brian couldn't lose. But he couldn't win, either, because no matter which he chose, he lost the opportunity to do the other. This was probably too hard a decision for a child at a year and a half. He would certainly learn, however, that his actions produce consequences.

Accountability is a buzzword in today's business world, probably because it's something that few adults have learned. Here, during this second year of life, is where you introduce the concept that a person is accountable for what he or she does, and that actions result in consequences.

If your child chooses to throw a tantrum, certain consequences follow. If your toddler chooses to test the limits, admonishment results every time.

In the "Great Food Fight" between Sara and Grandma described in Chapter 2, Grandpa finally put his foot down. "Enough of this. If she doesn't want to eat . . ."

"But Phil! She'll starve. She doesn't eat enough to—"

"Then she starves. If she doesn't want to eat, she gets down out of her high chair. But she doesn't come back later."

"But Phil—"

"That's it. I'm sick of the constant nagging."

Sara now had a choice. Eat or leave. In a sense, it was an experiment in trial and error imposed upon her from the outside. But it was also a valuable lesson in cause and effect, action and consequence. Sometimes she chose to get down from the table, irritating Grandma to no end. Sometimes she stayed and played. Occasionally she ate something. In every case she experienced a result from her action.

How effective would the lesson be? Only as effective as its enforcement. If Grandpa relented, the lesson would be muted. Fortunately, he did not. Consistency is everything.

There is a lag time between when the limits are set and when the toddler quits testing them consistently. Sometimes this lag period can last for weeks or months or even for years. To present an efficient, effective lesson, Grandpa must maintain his edict long enough (we're talking months now) that Sara can experience the full range of results from her choices—everything from premature hunger, to satiation, to seeing the frustration in Grandma.

"Full range" means that not all results and lessons are negative. Many times there are happy results, too, and you can make even more.

Enjoy Fun and Laughter Along with the Difficult Times

Somehow, for toddlers "fun" and "mess" are synonymous. For example, there was our Matthew's second birthday party. Vicky made two cakes, one for Matthew and one for the rest of the guests. She gave Matthew his cake and invited him to go at it—get as messy as he wished.

Then she looked at me and said, "Join him, Paul."

Me? Get cake all over me? A man of (ahem) considerable years? An educated adult, a professional, a . . . I was struck by how hard this was for me. I had to really work at giving myself permission to get messy. I was afraid of my image, my clothes, the floor—a whole number of things. But while I finally forced myself to get down and dirty, it came naturally to two-year-old Matthew.

It wouldn't now! My orderly son is into cars and computers these days—adult things. He'll be entering junior high before long. That moment would not work now. It had to be then, at two, or never. I'm glad it was then that it happened, that we both abandoned ourselves to the moment. It remains one of the highlights of his childhood for both of us.

Probably, "mess" and "fun" are linked so closely because children learn as much by touch and taste as they learn by eye and ear. Jenny intuitively figured that out as she took her Sara for walks. Jenny had seen a million butterflies, carefully sidestepped around a million puddles, rubbed the noses of a thousand horses, watched a hundred rabbits hop across the lawn down at the park, and picked a bezillion dandelions.

But Sara had not. All that was brand-new and good fun. And Jenny had the good sense to rediscover it with Sara. "Look! There's another butterfly! A swallowtail."

"Wow, Sara, that's fun!" she exclaimed as the toddler splashed a stick into a mud puddle. The baby got wet, yes. And when she stomped in it with a foot she got wetter. So what? The feel, the sensation, was all part of the lesson.

Let yourself see the world anew through your child's eyes. As you become involved in the world, your child will appreciate it more because you, the parent, are investing yourself. Remember that at the end of the experience, it's not the butterfly or the puddle after all; it's the relationship. Relationships are everything.

If that is so, what about others? Are Mommy and Daddy enough? How crucial is it for toddlers to be with others their own age?

Socializing with Nobody

"It's eerie. She sits here talking to this doll for minutes at a time." Jenny watched Sara at play in the pediatrician's waiting room.

Shauna Moore grinned. "All kids do that. My Afton

is starting to too. They use their imaginations to figure out the world."

"Yeah, but the doll doesn't even have a face! What's eerier, Sara can't talk."

As Sara and Brian expand their background of information enough to be able to imagine things, their imaginations take an ever more prominent role in figuring out the world around them. Also, they think symbolically for the first couple of years. Things don't have to be what they are; they need only represent what the child wants them to represent.

Sara's doll, her favorite companion, is a good example.

Sara's doll wears calico. Made of muslin, the doll had painted features once, but they washed off during the doll's first trip through the laundry. Jenny was devastated, but Sara did not seem to mind a bit.

What do we believe Sara sees with the doll? First, the doll is not a confidante; it simply represents a companion. The material object offers nothing more than a focus for the imagination. For the next few years, if Sara wants to iron like Mommy she can use a toy iron that looks like an iron, or she can use a building block. It will make no difference, for both toys, regardless of the degree of realism, will merely represent an iron.

So if you want to play trucks and you have no truck, you can pick up a toy car or a block or a beanbag, say "This is a truck," and it will be an adequate truck. By grade school, Sara will outgrow this symbolic imagining and need realism in her toys. Then they will have to look like what they are supposed to be. For now, it's symbolic all the way.

When Sara talks to the faceless (but not lifeless) little doll, she is learning about the world. In this way, toddlers are exactly like scientists. They amass data through observation, then they build a thesis to explain the data. Sara is a keen observer of everything that goes on. Remember that in a sense, she is viewing the world in slow motion, or more precisely, reduced motion—a slower time awareness. Also, toddlers like Sara are global observers in that they can see the whole scene without focusing on any one aspect. So Sara observes a lot.

Now she sorts out everything she has seen, heard, smelled, and tasted. She builds a theoretical world in her imagination. To test the question, "Is this what the real world is actually like?" she will play out the scenario. Still essentially without verbal skills, she must think by doing.

For instance, Sara is not able to picture her doll in its doll bed. She will lay the doll in the bed. *There*. Almost immediately she takes it out and goes off to do something else with it. This is not just short attention span. She is thinking about the doll in various aspects, so she must place it in those aspects.

Finally, we now understand that to a toddler, there is no line at all between the world of the imagination and the factual world. Reality and fantasy are equally real. That's hard for us stodgy old adults to grasp; for so many years, *You must tell the truth!* has been pounded into us, and fantasy is divorced from truth. In the next year, from ages two to three, the toddler will tell you some absolute whoppers and insist that they're true. To the child, they will be.

Jenny nodded. "Five minutes after Mom swatted her,

I saw Sara spanking her doll. So she was just playing out her experience, making sense out of it. Neat!" She grinned. "Instant replay with color commentary."

Often, in informal settings such as a dinner meeting, a worried parent will sidle up to me and ask, "Um, I'm not sure how to say this, but, um, my kid has this imaginary friend. It's, um, it's a horse." The real question is, *Is my kid loopy as a carnival ride?*

I'm always glad to provide the answer: "Perfectly natural. Don't think a thing of it." Very small children socialize freely with inanimate dolls and stuffed animals. Imaginary friends provide social scenarios in a nonthreatening setting the child can fully manipulate. It's a learning method, not an anomaly. It is just barely beginning in this one- to two-year period. In fact, in some children it will not appear until next year. It will flourish during the preschool years.

Socializing with Mom and Dad

When Tom took Brian with him to work one day his office coworkers thought he was nuts. "The kid's how old? Nineteen months? What's he going to remember about this place? It's a dump."

You know, Brian never noticed that the carpet was frayed and the walls needed painting. He remembered Daddy's work station and the wonderful assortment of things to handle and do. Scribble on paper. Staple things. Stamp with the stamp. The world is an amazing place to a child of nineteen months.

Mommy and Daddy are complex individuals with diverse interests in a variety of venues. It is a valuable thing for toddlers to see their parents in roles other than house-keeper, caregiver, and bedtime story reader. Again at a nonverbal level, the lesson becomes, *There is a great deal to life. My horizons are without limit.* Of course, Brian had no idea that there were such things as horizons. But that didn't stop him from expanding them.

Lessons abound as the parents model a variety of roles. Marsha sang in the choir on alternate Sundays. Tom was an usher at church. Once in a while he carried Brian on one arm as he handled the offering plate. Marsha took Brian along to the library and her favorite needlework shop.

Brian had no interest in needlework other than to play with yarn scraps. He had scant interest in the library, in fact. Those places took on meaning not intrinsically but because Mommy was interested in them. Mommy's and Daddy's interests expanded Brian's horizons, and Brian's expanding understanding of the variety and complexity of the world expanded the images of Mommy and Daddy. There was a cross-fertilization there, you see, that meant important, positive learning.

Accompanying parents is one thing. What about socializing with others?

Socializing with Others

When Brian Jasper's great-aunt Lyddie spoke, grown men quailed. Buxom and amply proportioned, she filled a room simply by entering it. If she had an opinion, she voiced it. And she never lacked an opinion. Well read, she knew about everything and could tell you how to do anything. She had her life in order, you'd better believe, and her mission now was to put everyone else's life in order.

She scared the bejabers out of little Brian, and out of his daddy too!

When Aunt Lyddie came to visit, she insisted upon making good friends with her dear grandnephew. Brian hid under the bed or behind Mommy. Aunt Lyddie insisted he ought to be placed on her lap. Brian insisted he wanted to be somewhere else. London, perhaps, or Boise. He was never going to get over his shyness, Aunt Lyddie emphasized, unless he was made to mix socially. "You don't want him to grow up timid, do you?"

What should Tom and Marsha's response be to Aunt Lyddie's firm insistence?

Tom wanted to hide under the bed with Brian, but Marsha was not intimidated. Marsha had grown up with Aunt Lyddie and her forceful ways. Marsha would act appropriately, politely but firmly refusing to force Brian into any social situation where he felt uncomfortable. And that, unfortunately, was any social situation involving Aunt Lyddie.

Marsha would be sending two messages thereby. One, she would tell Brian, *Your feelings have value. They are worth protecting.* By extension that message would become, *You have value.* Also, Marsha would be showing Brian that there are a lot of different kinds of people in the world, and he doesn't have to relate to all of them.

Even if Brian were naturally shy, as Aunt Lyddie suggested, forcing him into a tight social situation would not improve his shyness. Not when he was just plain scared of that big, loud lady. At three years, shyness might begin to be a problem. At eighteen months it is not.

Playmates—peers—are another matter.

When little Sara, in her frilly Sunday dress, arrived at the church nursery, Tony, aged two, was already there. Tony was playing with a truck. Sara needed that truck. *Now.* Tony gave up the truck and went to the sandbox. Then Sara needed to play with the truck in the sandbox. She evicted Tony by pushing him out. When she heard about it, Jenny could not believe it. Sara was never this way at home.

Many parents ask me, at seminars and workshops, how they can help their toddlers make friends. Frankly, they can't. What they are asking is essentially, "How can I get my toddler to play with other children without struggling over toys, hitting, and arguing?" Like Jenny, parents are shocked and amazed at their toddler's violent antisocial tendencies. But toy struggles and arguments are normal between children of this age. Below the age of three, children aren't really capable of playing cooperatively with others. They are still too busy learning about themselves and their nuclear family. They are not mature enough—not socially sophisticated enough—to develop relationships with peers. Instead, children this age will engage in what we call parallel play. They play side by side, usually in similar activities, without actual interaction or give-and-take.

Not that "take" isn't in their vocabulary. "Mine!" peppers their speech, and selfishness permeates their interactions.

Don't worry. Friendships with peers are not that important for toddlers of this age. When contact with peers becomes necessary, as it is at day care or in a nursery, structured play times must be *aptly supervised*.

Socialization in Today's Cruel World

When I was growing up, it was very important that children show respect to their elders and obey adults. You obeyed your parents, your teachers, the librarian, the gas-station attendant, and perfect strangers. You minded your manners and behaved.

Those days are no more. Please, please do not teach your children obedience!

Strong advice. Let me elaborate by example. In a city in Oregon, a teenager, a burly kid, saw a man carry a struggling child across a shopping-center parking lot. The teen ran to them and confronted the man. The man said he was taking his unruly son home. The boy, about four, screamed lustily that this was not his daddy.

Had the teen been taught to obey and respect elders, he would have backed off. Had the four-year-old been taught to obey, he would not be kicking and screaming, for the man repeatedly warned him to be quiet. Fortunately, the teen followed his gut feeling and insisted the man put the boy down. The fellow did—and ran. The teen had foiled an abduction by a man who, it was subsequently learned, had abducted and molested other small children.

Statistically, by far the most common molesters of small children, however, are not strangers. They are friends and relatives. These are the very people we think we ought to be teaching our children to obey.

Sexual abuse happens to infants. It happens to children aged one to two. No child is safe these days.

Marsha didn't even want to think about it. "I'll just have to keep an eye on him. I don't want to scare Brian with dire threats and stories. I don't want to make him afraid of everyone. No. Huh-uh."

Tom and Marsha taught Brian to stay out of the street; still, Brian did not fear streets. They taught him to handle dogs gently without scaring him in the process. Likewise, they could teach him important lessons that would protect him from abuse without making him afraid of people. Here are some of the lessons they would emphasize:

• *Body parts covered by swimsuits are special.* A child one to two years old has no concept of modesty and certainly no notions of sexuality. For small children, therefore, what a bathing suit covers is about as good a definition of private parts as any.

Who can touch those parts? A select few when Mommy or Daddy are present. Nobody when they aren't. Keep the rules very simple.

• *Yell and tell.* Abusive friends and relatives are expert at manipulating children. They know how to keep the kid silent. They use threats. "I'll hurt your Mommy if you say anything." "I'll kill your puppy." "This is our secret. If you say anything, I'll do bad things." The abuser may brandish a weapon. Usually, though, coercion is achieved, not by threatening the child, but by cajoling.

Emphasize to a child, even the youngest child, never to believe threats. Real friends and good relatives do not make threats. They do not keep secrets. Later, only Mommy and Daddy will keep secrets and those will be happy secrets that make you feel good, like birthday surprises. At this age, *no secrets* is rule enough. Tell. Always tell.

Abusers do not perpetrate their crime once and call it quits. Almost all abuse is repeated and repeated. That is what makes telling so important. It is the only way to stop abuse, which otherwise will extend across years.

Emphasize it: *Never keep a secret, no matter what the person says.*

Yell and tell. Tell, tell, tell.

I cannot emphasize enough the obverse side of this advice: *The parents then have a mutual obligation to believe.*

• *No matter what, it's not the child's fault.* Children suffer global guilt anyway; that means whatever happens, whatever goes wrong, they feel guilt and responsibility. This particular point won't mean too much yet at age one to two. It will bear incredible importance to older children. It will have to be drummed in over and over: *It is not your fault! No matter what you did or think you did, the adult [or older child] is the responsible party. The adult [or older child] is to blame. The fault is not yours. It never was.*

More complex rules can be provided to older children who have a more complex worldview. For a toddler, keep it very simple. Older children will benefit greatly by playacting "what if." What if a stranger calls to you from an open car window? What if a friend wants to touch your bathing-suit parts? What if . . . ? The one-year-old's background of experience and his or her worldview are not expansive enough yet to permit adequate imagination games.

Sexual abuse and other demented perpetrations have always been with us. But they are a particularly nasty fact of life in this day and age. Tom and Marsha cannot protect Brian fully enough to guarantee his freedom from danger. They should begin anti-abuse training even at this early age.

They can take comfort in the fact that pedophiles are very good at identifying lonely children, children who lack attention or affection. They then provide the attention and the affection in return for cooperation. One of your primary defenses against exploitation of your child will be nothing more than to provide ample attention and affection at home.

4. OUT OF THE MOUTHS OF BABES

LANGUAGE DEVELOPMENT

O LORD, our Lord,
How excellent is Your name in all
the earth,
Who have set Your glory above the
heavens!
Out of the mouth of babes and
nursing infants
You have ordained strength . . .

PSALM 8:1–2

The date: 1695. In a tiny parish in Lincolnshire, England, Susanna Wesley carried a heavy load of woe. A careless housemaid had dropped her baby girl, permanently crippling the child. Her son, Sammy, her firstborn, was quite obviously not right because at five years old, he still had not spoken his first word. Not a one. *Everyone knows if a child does not speak by three, he's not right in the head,* the neighbors whispered behind her back.

Woe upon woe, now Sammy was missing. He had wandered off.

The neighbors might be gossips, but they were good-hearted people. The whole village spread out, seeking Sammy—off by the rookery, in the marshes and ditches, up and down the lanes.

Distraught, Susanna sat on the windowsill watching the golden evening light on the grass outside. She burst aloud, "Oh, Sammy, Sammy! Where are you?!"

"I am here, Mother." Fully formed words, well articulated.

Out from beneath the floor-length tablecloth the little

boy crept. He had fallen asleep under the family table. And he chose that moment to speak his first words.

Nothing at all was wrong up in Sam Wesley's head. He became a noted scholar and eventually an Oxford dean. His brothers, John and Charles, entered history with their Methodist movement. In fact, a golden tongue seemed to run in the family. John's preaching converted thousands, and we still sing some of Charles's hymns today.

Little Samuel Wesley notwithstanding, how a child develops linguistically is generally regarded as a barometer of how well the child is developing as a whole. Within broad parameters, a child's intelligence seems to closely parallel language capabilities. This is no accident. The development of language skills is crucial to the development of other skills as well, especially cognitive thinking and social skills.

The Language Advantage: Helping Your Child Learn to Speak

I would venture to say that the more you work with a small child to encourage language growth, the bigger the leg up on life you give that child. So many other growth factors depend upon language.

Also, communication for its own sake is vitally important.

"Tell me about it," Tom Jasper said, bouncing his baby, Brian, who was laughing. "I remember when he was first born, and we didn't have a clue about what might be bugging him when he cried. How many times did we say, 'If only he could tell us what's wrong.' Before long, he'll be able to.''

To an extent. But learning always exceeds the ability to communicate it. For many years (sometimes a lifetime) the child will know far more than he or she can articulate. There are, you see, two facets of communication: comprehension (the receiver part) and articulation (the transmission part). Small children comprehend language well before they learn to speak it.

Comprehension

It sounds like a question from one of those government scandals: How much does a baby know, and when does he or she know it? We're learning all manner of amazing answers to this question.

Evidence abounds that language comprehension begins nearly at birth—perhaps even before. Voice recognition certainly happens very early. It is known that a baby whose deaf parents used sign language learned to sign "milk" at age three months. We do know that actual verbal communication lags a year or more behind comprehension. This is probably because verbalization requires so many intricate skills to come together in one place at one time to articulate certain sounds out of thousands of possible sounds—a daunting task.

Consider the babies in cultures other than ours. The infant or toddler accompanies Mommy all day, everywhere. On their travels, Mommy chats with the neighbors, haggles with a merchant, coos sweet nothings when Baby feels upset, tells Daddy about their day . . . The baby spends the day awash, not just in one voice, but in many, listening to a number of different people articulate one or more languages in a variety of ways.

How unfortunate that in our culture, Baby may hear only a couple of voices. Even more unfortunate, until Baby becomes verbal, a lot of parents don't bother to converse with the child at all. After all, they reason, why talk to a kid who can't talk?

You talk to a kid who can't talk because that kid is blotting up the vicissitudes of the mother language from day one. The baby is learning to speak many months before his or her lips, tongue, jaw, larynx, lungs, diaphragm, and brain get their act together enough to work in concert. For the first six months of life, babies can reproduce just about any sound and nuance possible in human speech. Their ear attunes to their mother tongue so accurately, however, that by the age of one year they will be able to comfortably pronounce only the sounds common to their principal language. The other sounds will have fallen by the way, mastered with difficulty later or not at all.

Sure, you should talk to your baby! Babble to your toddler, and use straight adult English (or your other primary language). Is the use of more than one language in a household confusing to a baby? Apparently not. Are some babblings better than others? To an extent. The bottom line in any case is to talk, talk, talk.

In the first book in this series, *My Infant,* I offered suggestions parents or childcare providers can use to communicate with their infants. Fine, you say, but what do you say to a one-year-old? As a general rule, it's not what you say but rather that you say it.

Read Books Aloud. There are so many wonderful children's books on the market today. Check out any number from the local library. However, be aware that children develop obsessions with favorite books. Long after the parent has become bored to unconsciousness with a story, the child will want it read again and again. So build a personal library for the child of however modest size.

Incidentally, as part of a survey many years ago in a major city, the top one-half of 1 percent of grade-school readers in the whole system were interviewed. The survey recorded that every single one of those fine readers learned to read before starting school. Further, every child interviewed reported that there were books in more than one room at home. There was a third point—every child interviewed watched the television series *M*A*S*H*, which was on during prime time then. The *M*A*S*H** connection I'm not sure about, except that the show was very well written. Parents who taught their children to read and who valued books enough to own many—that connection I am certain about.

There is absolutely no substitute for a parent's taking the child into his or her lap (a powerful symbolic statement of security and love) and reading a storybook (an equally powerful evocation of mythic communication we're only beginning to grasp).

Think of the lesson in articulation something as simple as *Goldilocks and the Three Bears* offers. Hear Daddy, as he cuddles the child protectively, reproducing Papa Bear's deep voice, then Mama Bear's medium voice, then Baby Bear's squeaky little voice. Hear the lilting cadence of the narrative. That is valuable language preparation for a child who cannot yet speak!

The Dr. Seuss books offer splendid training on the sorting and analysis of similar sounds. Later, when the child is older, he or she will love the wacky nonsense. At age one year, the wacky nonsense is perfectly normal, but the rhythm and the language lesson fascinate. A field biologist friend who wanted to read an ornithological treatise for his work dragged his one-year-old into his lap and proceeded to read a monograph on the *Trochilidae* (that's hummingbirds) aloud. It was the language, you see. Even though there was not a picture in the whole book, the kid bought it.

"To a point," the biologist said with a grin. "She fell asleep during the technical discussion of egg size."

Reproduce Babble. If a person repeats every word you say, you become annoyed immediately and infuriated eventually. Not so a baby. When Mommy or Daddy talks to Baby face-to-face, faithfully reproducing the sounds Baby makes, it is no mockery. The baby is not only delighted, but learning. *I make a* brbrbr *sound with* aaaah. *I know how it sounds when I do it. And there is how it sounds when Mommy does it.*

That's important information. The child has a long road ahead, and knowledge of how others perceive the sounds Baby makes will help immensely when the sounds are shaped into words.

On the other hand:

Avoid Correcting Your Child's Speech. If the child is hearing the right sounds and being spoken to with normal syntax, the child will reproduce the language properly as soon as he or she is able. Correcting pronunciation will avail nothing and may bring discouragement. Communication is a continuing process.

Says Tom Jasper proudly, "Brian is already saying 'scissors' and 'sugar.' Of course, at the moment, both words come out 'shoo-shoo.' "

Now what would be the message to Brian if Tom said, "No, Brian. That's not *shoo-shoo*. That's *sugar*"? Brian knows perfectly well the difference between sugar and scissors. He'll get it right as soon as he can. But notice that even his faulty pronunciation got the concept across. Tom knew what Brian was talking about. In short, communication had been achieved.

A response on Tom's part, "Sugar! Yeah!" would have sufficed to tell Brian that Daddy, indeed, understood Brian's attempt. Brian's try at communication was successful. That knowledge would get Brian much farther down the language road in the long run.

Talk. Narrate. "Hey, there's my Sara! Let's go see what's in the fridge!" Jenny has just walked in the door, home from work at the fast-food restaurant. She scoops up Sara and they head for the kitchen.

Jenny, with Sara under her arm, explores the refrigerator. "Peanut butter. Why not? Oh, good. There's some chocolate milk left. Do you want some too Sara?"

Sara, of course, cannot yet answer verbally. But with that question, Sara has been placed right in the middle of the action. Jenny continues a commentary as she drops Sara into her high chair, finds a table knife, and spreads peanut butter on little squares of bread. She pours milk into two plastic glasses, all the while talking about what she's doing.

Sara may not be saying a word, but the communication between them—Jenny's narrative and Sara's comprehension—is sweeping them both along. When Jenny holds out a bit of peanut-butter bread, Sara grabs it eagerly. Sara drinks her chocolate milk as Mommy drinks hers. Sara may well vocalize her babble of the moment. Jenny responds. Sara takes a few more peanut-butter morsels, licking her fingers off. The tongue coordination that licking needs is good exercise.

Remember that this is the little baby who refuses to eat for Grandma. At the moment, in her own eyes, she and Mommy are not really eating. They are engaged in a grand adventure of communication, and the peanut butter is not an end; it is a sidelight. The communication could just as well be in regard to a walk in the park or a book being read or the laundry (Jenny often narrates her actions as she washes or folds laundry). No matter. The communication, the sharing, is the thing. Relationship. It all comes back to relationship.

Sara was Jenny's only child, and once Jenny got off work, she could spend time with her baby. Brian was the Jaspers' only child. What about when the one-year-old is a second or third child?

Usually, if the space between the first child and the next is such that a newborn demands Mommy's time just as the toddler is starting to speak, the toddler's language development suffers. Kids need an awful lot of time in the saddle, as it were, talking and being talked to. Mommy has twenty-four hours in a day, and the new baby is filling many of them. She simply cannot give her emergent orator the time required.

Language Preparation

What do you hope to accomplish by reading and talking to your child? I suggest these goals are relevant between ages one and two. They will change later.

For now, you want to instill in your toddler these lessons:

Communication gets positive results. Be it attention from you or a need fulfilled, communication achieves a desired result. Crying, gesturing, and speaking are all means of gaining a desired response.

Using the voice is pleasurable. Shauna Moore's Afton is deaf. Shauna didn't know it at first. For the first six months, Afton babbled and cooed like any other baby. But gradually the verbalizations grew less and less. Shauna ran a few rough-and-ready hearing tests of her own. She called Afton's name at various pitches of voice while standing just out of view. Afton's head did not turn toward Mommy's voice. When a neighbor dog barked suddenly, practically in Afton's face, the baby did not jump or respond as if startled. Afton did not turn in curiosity toward clapping hands.

Shauna took her to a hearing specialist.

The reduced verbalization, at a time when verbalization usually increases and becomes more varied, was the sure tip-off. Deaf children do not feel the pleasure of hearing their own voice. This feel-good feedback is so crucial to language development that they stop verbalizing all together.

Other people use language successfully. We take this goal for granted. Of course other people use language. Everyone knows that. But when you're a year old, that's not a given. It's something to be learned.

Afton did not know about language, let alone that it was useful. Immediately, Shauna began learning sign language.

"Boy, that's hard," Shauna confided. "I'm looking at this propped-up book and trying to figure out the gestures, and it's *hard!* I can't tell if I'm doing it right. I enrolled in a course at the community college, but it won't start for another three months. I wanted to do this right away, you know?"

Shauna acted wisely. Afton might never know the spoken language, but she was at that window of opportunity where the concept of language in general—not just speaking—must be learned. It had to happen right now. Sign language is just as valid a means of communication as any spoken tongue and would serve Afton well.

Groping her way, Shauna felt the same frustrations and fears any beginning communicator feels. *Am I doing it right? Will she understand? It's so difficult!*

Incidentally, sign language is also good in certain situations where there is a handicap other than deafness. For instance, teachers of Down syndrome children suggest that parents employ sign language in addition to spoken communication. Signing exact English is the way to go in this instance. The child sees a manual version of what the ears are hearing (hearing is reduced in many Down children anyway), and comprehension improves because the message is coming from two separate sources. Also, because certain handicapped children, Down children among them, often have difficulty forming words, sign language provides them with an alternate means of being understood.

The lessons are learned, the goals in sight. The day arrives, usually in this span between first birthday and second, when baby begins communication in earnest. That involves articulation—speaking intelligibly—and some of the rules will change.

Articulation

A swirl of pigeons leaves the bronze head of Thomas Jefferson and alights at the booted feet of Brian Jasper. He cackles with delight. "Bur! Bur!"

"They *are* birds! Look at those birds!" Marsha holds the popcorn bag down so Brian can grab a handful. He tosses it a good eighteen inches. With a flurry, the pigeons, strutting and cooing, promenade before him.

"More!" Brian twists to reach the popcorn.

Brian has achieved two-way communication. But just now he isn't interested in communication as such. He's interested in feeding the pigeons.

Brian has stepped over a giant threshold, and neither he nor his parents noticed. At first, reproduction of sounds was an end in itself. Now, communication is the end, and sounds are only a means. He has begun to communicate without thinking about it. His thoughts are all elsewhere. By analogy, a beginning cyclist has to concentrate on riding the bike. Before long, the cycling comes more or less automatically and the cyclist is concentrating on the destination or an unrelated conversation or the surrounding scene.

For most children, this giant step, as well as articulation, begins between the ages of one and two. The threshold passes unnoticed because the mechanics of comprehension have already been in place for some time. Communication, in one direction at least, is old hat.

As the child enters into this second year, he or she already recognizes a rich variety of words, more than a hundred and fifty by most counts. A one-year-old's understood vocabulary usually consists of the following basic words plus variations:

Mommy	*hug* or
Daddy	*Give me a hug* or
cracker	*Hug me*
cookie	*water*
dog or *doggy*	*drink*
cat or *kitty*	*Come here*
bye-bye	*Sit down*
hi	*Stop that*
ball	(other simple commands)
juice	*dance*
hug	*walk*
kiss or	*peek-a-boo*
Give me a kiss or	*patty-cake*
Kiss me	*book*
throw	*socks, shoes*
me	*pants, shirt*
no no	(other articles of clothing)
feet, hands	*chair* or *high chair*
eyes, ears	*burp*
(other body parts)	*uh-oh*

These are the words of the average child's world. A child raised on a ranch in New Mexico may know breeds of cattle and horses by name. A child who grows up on a houseboat or a live-aboard sailboat may know what the anchor is and know he wears a flotation device instead of a baby T-shirt. Vocabulary varies with circumstances.

By his or her second birthday, the average two-year-old's vocabulary has expanded dramatically to include:

> *horse, cow,* and other familiar animals. The vocabulary of a child of two who grew up just outside Yellowstone National Park included *elk.*
>
> *phone, keys, blanket*
>
> *milk, apple, cereal, bottle*
>
> *bed, blanket, bunny* (or some other favorite stuffed toy)
>
> *hat, coat, jacket, sweater*
>
> *teeth* or *Brush your teeth*
>
> *hair* or *Comb your hair*
>
> simple questions like: *Where is (are) . . . ?* and *Do you want (a cookie, a cracker, to get out of your crib)?*
>
> simple commands like: *Go get . . . ; Let's go . . . ; Find me . . . ; No, don't touch . . . ; Stop that; Shut the door; Turn on/off the light; Close the door; Put away your toys; Let's clean up*
>
> terms relevant to the world outside: *car, grocery cart, gas station,* and perhaps *bicycle* or *stroller*
>
> day care terms

At two, as at every other age, the child knows far more words than he or she can use off the top of his or her head. The toddler is likely to take a crack at handling any or all of the words listed above, but in practical day-to-day life, don't expect a full use of vocabulary. You don't use half the words you know; neither does the toddler.

New Speaker, New Rules

With a new speaker in the house, a person in love with this intricate and marvelous skill, all the rules change. Well, a lot of them do.

Big, hulking Aunt Lyddie smiled at Brian with teeth the size of tent pegs. "You know my name, don't you, Brian?"

Brian nodded shyly, his ear pressed against Mommy's leg.

"Can you say my name, Brian?"

Another little nod.

"Well, take your fingers out of your mouth—there, like a big boy, and tell me my name."

Clearly and distinctly, Brian said, "Moose."

New Rule 1: What your baby hears, the world will hear. Count on it. Tom was most unwise to call the woman behind her back a name he would not call her to her face. Assume that any word you speak will ostensibly find an audience of hundreds. Season your speech accordingly.

New Rule 2: Weigh cuteness carefully. It's cute now, but will it be when the child is six or twelve? Words, actions, and even, to some people, blasphemies may sound precious when coming from the mouth of a toddler. Reward or condemn those words according to whether you want to hear them from the mouth of your grade-schooler. You do a profound disservice to a small child who is rewarded for something on one occasion and excoriated for it on another.

New Rule 3: Interpret when the child needs it. At dinner, Aunt Lyddie wrinkled her nose. "What is he saying? It sounds obscene."

"That was 'potato,' Aunt Lyddie. He wants some more mashed potatoes." Marsha plopped a tiny blob of potatoes on Brian's plastic dish. "More gravy?"

He bobbed his head.

Aunt Lyddie frowned reprovingly. "He should be saying 'please' and 'thank you.'"

Marsha smiled. "He will. He will."

"Really, Marsha, you shouldn't give him anything unless he says 'please' and 'thank you.' Now what did *that* mean?"

"Shee!" Brian repeated, waving his spoon.

Marsha frowned. "On your potatoes?"

"Shee!"

"He wants cheese on his potatoes." Marsha sprinkled a bit of shredded cheddar on top of the gravy.

Brian's spoon went flying over the side. He leaned over to look at it and uttered the classic phrase of every toddler: "Uh-oh!"

By interpreting in clear English Brian's bold attempts at speaking, Marsha delivered an important lesson. She told him, *Your communication is valued; you are valued.* And also, interpreting when necessary reduces the frustration the child experiences during this first overture into the outside world of communication.

Relatives who do not visit frequently, such as grandparents, will find interpretation of special help. They're not used to the toddler's approximations.

New Rule 4: Babble is out. Once the child begins forming words, repeating babble is no longer necessary. Now the child needs to hear how the word is really pronounced.

Nor does Jenny need to continue prattling on about nothing, narrating her actions as she goes. At this age, babbling and prattling send the child a message that communication has no purpose or has no real strength.

From now on, you and your child can enjoy a far superior form of talking—actual two-way communication. The old is left behind. All is new.

New Rule 5: Silly games and songs are in. "Must I?" Tom Jasper looked with disdain at the prospect of having to do the hokeypokey or play ring-around-the-rosy or . . .

"Have at it, Big Guy," Marsha said with a smirk. "I'd love to help, but I gotta go make dinner."

Toddlers need lots of verbal repetition, not just of words but of sounds and phrases. The really useful songs and ditties repeat sounds over and over. "Old MacDonald's Farm" with its incessant E-I-E-I-O is a perfect example. The simple game of patty-cake offers an excellent combination of repetitive sound and physical movement.

But silly songs and games serve a more fundamental purpose than language mastery, important as that is. They bring Mommy and Daddy together with the child at the child's level of interest. That's called "bonding" in modern parlance. It builds family as nothing else can. It also builds the child's self-esteem and the parents' affection. *Relationship.*

Relationship, relationship, relationship. There are other things to watch, now that your child's pursuit of language is roaring along full cry.

Television

Like many small children, Jenny grew up spending hours in front of the TV set. She had her favorite programs, of course. Now while she was at work, her mom used the television set with Sara the way she used to with Jenny.

Sara, though, did not sit still for TV. If she watched at all, her attention span was limited to moments. Her grandma actually got frustrated by her lack of success in keeping Sara quiet with the electronic baby-sitter.

Toddlers between age one and two can get by just fine without television. Any aid to language development that educational television might provide is by no means necessary. Television viewing promotes physical inactivity, the last thing a toddler needs. The child does better with no television at all.

Background Noise

A very nice lady once told me that she didn't watch the soaps herself, but she left the set on to entertain her dog. For whatever reason, a great many homes keep the radio or television set (sometimes both!) running nearly all day, whether or not anyone is paying attention. This background noise is both addicting and distracting, particularly for a small child.

Children absolutely must have generous blocks of free,

unstructured time. It's not loafing. It's not wasted. They use that time to work out problems through play, process information, and let the clutter of random observations sift out into understandable patterns. Background noise seriously detracts from those important processes.

If you need background sound, choose quiet instrumental music. Vocals will interfere with children's emergent thought processes. In fact, vocals also interfere with yours.

Listening

"Of course I listen to Sara!" Jenny's mom protested. "I can tell when she really needs something and when she's just jabbering at me."

Just jabbering at me.

How sad.

I deal with hundreds of troubled children. To help them not just temporarily but for a lifetime, I don't preach or scold or cajole. Ninety-nine percent of the time I *listen.*

As you sit and listen for a while to a child, even a very small child, and watch him or her play, you soon gain an understanding of what is going on inside that tiny head. Listen long enough, and you know every dynamic in the child's life and in the parents'.

Listening is a skill few have mastered, probably because it seems too simple a thing to do. In fact, a large part of my help consists of teaching both children and their parents simply to listen to each other. Really listen. Truly hear what is said.

There are ways to sharpen your listening. With your

improved perceptiveness you will be able to read your toddler much better and help the child grow much better.

Does little Sara realize that her grandma is not really listening to her? You bet. Does it have an accumulative effect on her? Of course. When Grandma tunes out, Grandma is saying, *Your interests don't count*. What Grandma perceives as jabbering is Sara's attempt to make sense of the world. Certainly it sounds like childish nonsense. From what background would Sara draw wisdom?

How Is Your Listening?

This casual little personal survey is designed to help you analyze your listening habits. It does not refer just to your listening habits with a small child but with everyone and everything—spouse, strangers, the person on the phone, background sounds.

1. Situations when I tune out:
   _____ The speaker is boring or not engaging.
   _____ Too much on my mind.
   _____ Distractions.
   _____ No real reason; I just do.

2. Situations when I cut off what I was listening to (such as interrupting or silencing the speaker, hanging up, turning off the radio or changing stations):
   _____ I disagreed with what I was hearing.
   _____ I was not interested in what I was hearing.
   _____ Something else required or invited my attention.

_____ No real reason. I just did.

3. Where I look when I am listening to a person face-to-face:
_____ In the person's eyes.
_____ At the person if possible.
_____ Near the person.
_____ At whatever else is interesting.

4. Methods I use when listening is important:
_____ Take notes of the main points.
_____ Tape the exchange or discourse.
_____ Ask questions, request clarification.
_____ Move in closer to the speaker or source.
_____ Repeat the points I hear.

5. For background or white noise I prefer:
_____ Television.
_____ Easy listening or soft rock.
_____ Soothing stuff: jazz, new age, or classical.
_____ Country/western or rhythm and blues.
_____ Something loud with a beat.
_____ Organic sound: falling water, seashore, frogs, birds.
_____ Nothing. Silence.
_____ Other.

6. I would estimate that I comprehend:
_____ 80 percent of what I hear.
_____ 50 percent of what I hear.
_____ 30 percent of what I hear.
_____ Let's face it. I'm not listening.

Now let's assume that you really are interested in developing strategies for listening better to your toddler (and secondarily, to everyone else as well). If you can truly listen to a toddler and hear what is being said (or attempted), you can listen to anyone. Believe me. I listen to kids all day. I know.

Taking the survey items in reverse order, statement 6 is a zinger. I didn't suggest 100 percent because people know that couldn't be the right answer. And yet, most folks honestly believe they comprehend nearly 100 percent of what they hear. The recognized answer by people who know? Maybe 30 percent, generally speaking. Trained listeners, such as investigative officers, psychologists, and lawyers, will reach or exceed 80 percent *on the job*. Off the job, they usually don't pick up much more than most other people do. Just about everyone, then, is a candidate for improving listening skills.

Think again about your answers in statements 1 and 2 on the survey. They give you a general idea of where your interests lie (and they don't always lie where you think they should). If you cut off people who are talking politics or making a sales pitch, you obviously aren't interested in spending your precious time with that sort of thing. If that is so, you may well feel the toddler's pitch is a waste of time as well. Examine your attitude in that regard. Let me assure you, no time spent really listening to a small child is wasted time. Not at all. That "irrelevant" babbling is extremely relevant and necessary to the child. By listening, you are helping the child grow in worldly wisdom, in language skills, and in socialization.

Be aware that tuning out may not be voluntary at

all. Some people, particularly children and adults with attention deficit disorder (ADD) tendencies, tune out whether or not they want to. It's organic. The brain jumps the track, and that is that. Analyze your reasons for tuning out, and the occasions when that happens. You may fall into that class of ADD people and others. If so, you will have to be prepared to realize when you're tuning out with a child and ask for a repeat of what was said, bringing your mind back to the child's matter at hand.

What is your favorite background noise? Silence actually is not the preferred answer if you have to listen in a noisy environment—in a large open office area, for example, or on the sales floor of a store. Then, white noise, which masks discordance with soothing tones and rhythm, will help your concentration.

When you're listening to a toddler, you're usually in a home environment or somewhere else reasonably pacific— a park, for example. Wherever that may be, make certain that any background noise is contributing to your concentration and not distracting you. Answering "television" to statement 5 is saying, in effect, "major distraction."

Your answers to 3 and 4 indicate that you really do try to listen; you've developed effective strategies and techniques. When talking with your toddler, looking at the child's eyes and face always improves retention. It also gives the child a strong nonverbal message: *You are an important individual.*

All the suggestions in statement 4 are good for improving your skills at listening. Of course, you are not going to tape record your toddler in order to seize every nuance, and I doubt you'll take notes. Those strategies are for when you can reasonably expect a pop quiz on Friday. But moving in closer—that is, dropping down to face-to-face level with the child—is an excellent ploy. With a toddler, picking up the kid so you can stand there eye to eye is just as good. To toddlers accustomed to being summarily scooped up, ground level and sky level are pretty much the same. So are asking questions and repeating what you hear. I strongly recommend both strategies. Not only will you hear your child better, you will be, again, sending the message that *You are important. I care.*

I suggest also these additional strategies when talking to your toddler:

Show active listening body language. That means look your speaker straight in the eye. Maintain an "open-body" position—no crossed arms or legs. Lean toward your speaker and nod when you understand something. Get down at the same level as your toddler. Can a small child pick up on those nonverbal cues? Certainly. Such gestures are innate—programmed into the human being, particularly in our culture, and discernible below conscious level even to your toddler. He or she will sense that you're really interested.

Practice reflective listening. Repeating what is said is called "reflective listening." When a toddler is doing the saying, it is also called "translating," or attempting to. Marsha did that when Brian was requesting cheese.

Check out feelings with a question. If you make an extra attempt to understand what the other person is feeling, your comprehension also improves. With kids it's easy to understand how they feel by asking.

"Are you mad at Daddy because he didn't buy you

that candy bar at the store?" For a toddler, you might even have to act out what mad looks like with a facial expression. If you hit the mark, validate your toddler's feelings. "It's okay to be mad at me. You know what? I get mad at people when they won't give me what I want too. But your mom is fixing dinner for us and you wouldn't be hungry enough to eat dinner if you ate that big candy bar."

Is your toddler going to understand all that fine reasoning? Probably not. The lesson you just provided was not on appetite and blood-sugar levels but on feelings, a much more important subject. *It's okay to have feelings, and it's okay to express them. Daddy values your feelings enough to talk about them.*

Listening skills, important as they are, certainly are not the only silver bullet to language learning. Along with listening, nothing helps a child master language better than simply spending time.

Put in the Time

The vast majority of parents in my counsel, fathers in particular, complain, "I want to spend time with my kid, and he won't have anything to do with me." He or she— son or daughter, the lament is the same. Unfortunately, the fathers saying this are invariably trying to get to know their kids at age twelve or into the teens. "You know, when the kid is finally getting interesting and you can talk about stuff," these dads might say. This is just when separation and individuation are entering the final lap of the childhood race. This is when the children are in their last great struggle to forge an identity for themselves, and they don't *want* to develop a close association with the parents at this stage of the game. Just the opposite. Now is when they are trying to distance themselves.

When the father should have been spending time with his child was back here in these first three years. This was when the child needed large chunks of Daddy's time—Daddy's in particular but Mommy's also, of course. Unfortunately, at age one or two the kid isn't especially interesting yet for a lot of fathers. No grasp of sports or cars, no intellectual linkage, no meeting of the minds.

Remember that even if the toddler achieves a splendid degree of language sophistication, able to spout an extensive vocabulary in good syntax, the child's intellectual level is still one year old. Beware of the trap of treating a child who talks like a three-year-old like a three-year-old. Chronological age during these three years is a lot better indicator of reality than is a surface sophistication.

It's difficult for an adult to shift mental gears enough to get down to a toddler's level of play and interest. It was particularly hard for me to relate well to my son, Matthew. I spent all day at the office carefully and attentively listening. I picked up on spoken and unspoken messages. I practiced all the techniques a good counselor practices. I drew lots and lots of pictures. I played a stultifying number of games of Candyland and Parcheesi with my young clients.

When I got home, what did Matthew need from his daddy? Concentration, listening, drawing pictures, playing games. But I was all washed out.

Most mommies and daddies are washed out when they get home from work, even if they aren't working with children all day. And yet, the child at this age requires the whole daddy and the whole mommy. You put your listening skills to full use. You give the child your full attention. If you do so now, during this golden age from one to two, you will accomplish two important objectives.

First, you will vastly improve your child's language skills. Vastly. The child needs linguistic interaction, give-and-take, and talking and hearing in order to build mastery. Only time spent talking to you and interacting with you on a verbal level will do that. No video, no magic formula, no "Five Quick Steps" can lead your child to language mastery. Only you. Only by spending time together.

Second, you will lay a foundation of closeness and trust that will pay its dividend up there at the other end of childhood. You, as Daddy or as Mommy, will not be coming to a counselor, lamenting, "My kid avoids me. I want to get to know my child." You and your child will be close enough that this final split will not be the wrenching break it so often becomes.

Consider your time spent now, listening to and talking with and being together, as the most important investment you will ever make.

The problem, of course, is that parents can never spend the kind of time with their toddlers that one would call ideal. The result is a great deal of anxiety, perhaps shame or perhaps transferred anger (getting angry at someone else who presumably deserves ire when the anger is actually generated by the parent's own sense of guilt or inadequacy).

In the next chapter, we'll explore how those emotions affect your child.

5. THE MYTH OF THE PERFECT PARENT

REDUCING PARENTAL ANXIETY

The joys of parents are secret;
and so are their griefs and fears.

FRANCIS BACON

Perhaps it was because of the time he got hit in the eye with somebody else's Frisbee, or maybe it was that he had once eaten tainted chicken and was sick for three days. Possibly it was because of the time he had to help the boss's wife carry her potato salad from the car to the picnic shelter and he dropped it. (Everyone else thought his *faux pas* was a blessing from God—or maybe even intentional—and they were ready to give him a medal [very privately], but the boss's wife was upset. She was jealously proud of her potato salad.) Whatever the reason, Tom Jasper used to hate company picnics. *Hate* them! But all that had changed; now he loved them.

Tom pulled Brian free of the carseat and slipped him into his baby backpack as Marsha dug her casserole out of the hatchback. This was going to be a great day. Tom set the backpack on the front fender, did his quick double-twist, and slipped the straps over his shoulders. With Brian picking at the short hairs on the nape of Tom's neck, they headed out across the grass to the group area.

Tom recalled warmly their arrival at the picnic last year,

when Brian was seven months old. Everyone cooed and purred over the baby. The women literally stood in line for a chance to hold him. And he was *big*. Brian had been the biggest baby at the picnic, and two of them were months older than he.

As Marsha took her food to the serving table, Tom joined his office mates over by the barbecue pit, modestly prepared for a similar triumph. Everyone greeted him, and he greeted everyone. No one asked to hold the baby. In fact, no one paid much attention to Brian. After a few minutes, Tom swung Brian off his back and pulled him out of the backpack. "Go run around a while, Big Guy."

Brian took off toward a sandpile where half a dozen tots were playing.

Tom frowned slightly and tried to disguise it as concentration. "Say, Harry. Isn't that your redhead?"

"Yeah. Seventeen months old, and look at him!"

Harry's redhead, two months younger than Brian, was bigger. Noticeably bigger. So was Harry's head. The guy grinned like he had just won the lottery.

A small blonde girl who Tom knew was a month or so younger than Brian began babbling to her mother nearby. Not babbling. Talking. Complete sentences. Clear enunciation. Eighteen months old. Brian's meager attempts at speaking, mostly screams, grunts, and vowel sounds, made Sylvester Stallone sound like a polished orator.

"Conner? Bring me a Pepsi, will you?" Tom recognized the mail-room clerk, a nice young woman with glasses and a quiet smile. Tom thought her husband's name was Bill, not Conner. *Oh*. Here came Conner with a can of Pepsi. Conner was a toddler, smaller than Brian.

Tom Jasper hated company picnics.

How Does My Child
Measure Up?

Tom Jasper was not alone in his pride and anxiety. Universally and naturally, parents compare their children to everyone else's, if only below conscious level. When their children appear superior, they privately gloat a bit or praise God or both. When the comparison is not favorable—and averages being what they are, half the time it won't be—anxiety sets in.

This parental anxiety can cause problems if it compels you to try to change your toddler into someone the child is not. I see that happen frequently.

Channeling anxiety differently, you can improve yourself as a parent. That is the response that leads to personal growth and healthy change for both you and your child.

Why do we worry when we set our youngster next to someone else's and decide ours fails to measure up? There are several underlying reasons.

Image

When Tom's company associates made over the infant Brian so freely, and when Brian came across as bigger and heavier than any other baby, Tom could not help but perceive himself as a superior father. Look what he sired! *Top of the line. It takes better-than-average genes to get a better-than-average kid.*

At a deeper level, the next generation is all that will

persist of this generation. A child is more than just a child. A child is the parent and the grandparent, extended through time. Genetically, a superior child means a better shot at glory through time. Someday.

Potential

Were Tom to admit his most personal dreams for his son's future, he would describe Brian as a doctor who went through college on a full athletic scholarship. Most dreams that parents have for their children require comparison all along the line. The winner of an athletic scholarship must triumph over his or her competitors. Brian will be forever rated and compared. It's only natural for hopeful parents to size up their child's potential from the beginning.

Investment

Tom and Marsha Jasper worked diligently for five years to conceive the baby that was Brian. Thus they had more invested in Brian both emotionally and financially than do many parents.

Jenny Lawton's Sara was the result of an accidental pregnancy, but Jenny had invested heavily already, with an even heavier investment to come. Jenny had put much of her high school life on hold. Her own potential as a skilled wage earner would be curtailed, major elements of her social life postponed or eliminated. Only by the grace of her parents' assistance did she complete high school. Not all girls are that fortunate.

It is natural to want an impressive return on investments so draining.

The Meaning of It All

At the company picnic, Tom discovered that his Brian no longer appeared to be the biggest or the best or the smartest. Did that mean the full scholarship was out and medical school was a forlorn hope?

It didn't mean a thing. The nature and temperament of toddlers are strong indicators of what they will be like someday. But the toddler at age one gives absolutely no hint of just where and how far he or she will go on the way to adulthood and beyond. There's many a save twixt birth and the grave, and also many a pitfall.

Tom Jasper knew in theory that his Brian was a unique child with unpredictable potential and that progress at age one hinged not upon Brian's standing against friends' kids but upon Tom and Marsha's efforts as parents. In practice, though, that bugbear of comparison kept slipping through.

Another comparison parallels this sizing up of the child: the sizing up of the parent. And it is just as much a spoiler as is comparison between children.

How Do I Measure Up?

Marsha Jasper plopped Brian down on the floor with his plate of lunch goodies in front of him. She sat on the sofa behind him and began to eat her lunch.

This was the monthly luncheon that Carrie Parker, one of the women in Marsha's birthing class, had organized. The eight who participated regularly alternated among each other's houses. This month, it was at Carrie's.

It was awfully easy to envy Carrie Parker. She was a great organizer and hostess. Her kid behaved. She maintained a firm but gentle control, even in the delivery room. She never had a bad hair day.

Here she came to the sofa in all her perfection, balancing her plate and a soft drink. She settled down softly beside Marsha. "Let Ed play hostess awhile. I'm hungry."

From the kitchen, her equally perfect husband called, "More iced tea, anyone?"

Marsha finished her bite of macaroni salad. "This lunch is delicious, Carrie." She watched Brian stuff his mouth with tiny fish crackers. His favorites.

A chorus of voices agreed with her compliment.

Suddenly, with a scream and yell, Carrie's girl and the Kanes's boy came toddling into the living room, the Parker cat stretched out between them like the rope in a grotesque tug-of-war.

"Lionel! Jamie!" Carrie hopped up from the sofa without spilling her food or anyone else's. "Put the kitty down! Muffin is not a play toy."

Jamie dropped her half. Carrie rescued the frazzled tabby from Lionel's determined grip. The cat streaked in frantic silence out the dining room door.

"Li'el want Muff'n," Jamie whined, as great, heart-tugging tears welled in her eyes. "Muff'n *my* kitty."

"That's right, honey," Carrie said, wiping the tears. "But you know what, sweetie? Muffin shouldn't be fought over. Muffin can hurt, can't she?"

Jamie's charming little head bobbed. And then the toddler did what toddlers do so well. She shifted her mood instantly from tears to sweetness. On stiff little legs, she wheeled and speed-walked after Lionel down the hall.

Marsha heard, "Noooo, my toys!" in the distance.

Carrie sighed, sat down, and picked up her plate. "Ed's turn."

His fish crackers gone, Brian scrambled to his feet and ran after the other two kids, kicking over his cup of juice in the process.

"Oh no!" Marsha pounced on the carpet, retrieved the glass, and began blotting at the juice with her napkin. "I'm so sorry, Carrie. Brian!"

"Sit and eat," Carrie advised as she herself sat calmly and ate. "Don't worry about it. It'll shampoo out."

Marsha returned to the sofa; her napkin was too soaked to be effective on the spill anymore. She was a successful college graduate, a library volunteer, a church secretary. Why did she feel so very inept next to Carrie's confidence? She could tell the answer even as she pondered the question. Carrie Parker always knew just what to do. She never got ruffled. She always looked good.

If ever there was a perfect parent, Carrie was it.

Nobody's Perfect

Once upon a time, almost everyone lived by the same set of rules: You got a job in order to support yourself and your family, you tried to get the kids through childhood without the help of a parole officer, college was not for everyone, and stress was the force heavy trucks placed upon bridges.

Somewhere, somehow, someone in the last thirty years

changed all those rules. Mysterious people we label as "they" told us that earning a living was no longer sufficient justification for a job. Now every job had to be a career, and it had to be meaningful and rewarding. Everybody's kid was expected to be better than average, college was a stepping-stone every person should use toward that meaningful and rewarding career, and women could have it all. Suddenly, being "just okay" was no longer okay enough. Parents, kids, homes, careers, possessions, leisure time, investments, pets, and automobiles—all had to be ideal. Also utterly safe. And also . . . and . . .

Unfortunately, we bought the line from start to finish and never paused to seriously question all those new and demanding *and totally unrealistic* expectations.

Anna Quindlen, a syndicated columnist for the *New York Times,* summed up the anxiety beautifully in her April 14, 1994 column. She cited a study from the Families and Work Institute that rated day care quality as surprisingly low. The study measured quality by examining the amount of time caregivers spent with children playing, doing puzzles, reading stories, and such. Ms. Quindlen quite accurately observed that she, as the mother of three small children, did not come near meeting the expectations the study placed upon outside caregivers. In other words, normal motherhood is inadequate.

And then, buried in the last third of her essay, she hit upon the crux of the matter and totally missed it. She wrote, "While the study of family day care showed that only about half the children were 'securely attached' to their caregiver, studies of attachment to mothers show, happily, a much higher number."

Attachment. As nice as all the games and puzzles and toys and playtime are, attachment is the one and only crucial concern. Can Anna Quindlen forge attachments during time spent, as she puts it, "Wheeling them around supermarket aisles talking to myself"? Yes. Talking to them, certainly. The question then settles down to, How perfect must a parent be?

How Close to Perfect Do I Need to Be?

In an important way, Marsha was justified in her expectations of perfection. Brian was a neat kid with immense potential, even if Tom didn't quite see him as comparing favorably with all other children. Brian deserved the best. "The best possible" and "perfect" have somehow become synonymous in our new Great Expectations culture.

Viewed realistically, "the best possible" and "perfect" are nowhere close to each other. Marsha hungered, not just for perfection in general, but more specifically for the image of the perfect parent. *Appearances.* It was no happenstance that Marsha envied Carrie's unruffled demeanor, every hair in place.

Most parents do. When they come to me, their child is in grade school or early high school. Something has gone dreadfully awry, literally forcing them into my office. And I find in them a common thread of profound shame and embarrassment. With their kid misbehaving, their own image of perfect parenting is shattered. I do not mean to suggest that they come to me for the sake of their image and not for their child's sake. No. But I do contend that the parental image is a part of the equation and usually a significant part.

Does it matter? Plenty. Parents place upon themselves the pressure to be perfect. That pressure translates downward to the child to be perfect. But a child is not perfect. No one is farther from perfection than a toddler, and no one is closer. For all the defiance and testing of this turbulent age, the child will never be more cooperative when he or she feels like cooperating, more happy to please, more open to learning. The last thing this little tyke needs is pressure to perform in ways the child often cannot understand.

What is naughty? What generates yelling? Too often that depends on whether one is in public or sequestered in the privacy of home. But home and public are the same thing to a one-year-old. So why do the rules change? Pressure.

How strong is your interest in your image? Every parent would love to say, "Very weak. The child is what matters." To which I say, "Amen." To assess your attitude, complete the following statements:

How Do I Think the World Perceives My Parenting?

1. I am most careful about my child's behavior:
_____ When we are around other people.
_____ When my in-laws and parents visit.
_____ All the time.

2. My children tend to misbehave more:
_____ When we are around other people.
_____ When they're with their grandparents.

_____ When they're tired and crabby.

3. The behavior of other people's children in grocery stores:
_____ Appalls me.
_____ Could be improved with firm discipline.
_____ Pretty much parallels my own kids' behavior.

4. Of the following, the best moment-to-moment indicator that I'm doing all right as a parent is:
_____ My child's behavior in public.
_____ My child's intelligence.
_____ My child's degree of relaxation.

5. Arrange statements _a_ through _h_ below in order of relative importance, making the most important statement number 1 and the least important statement number 8.

   I think the worst or most dangerous behavior problem for a child this age is:

a. _____ Screaming, tantrums in public.
b. _____ Screaming, tantrums anytime.
c. _____ Active disobedience; indicating refusal with words and gestures ("No!" Stomping foot, etc.).
d. _____ Passive disobedience; simply not doing it.
e. _____ Doing the opposite of an order (such as running away when told to come).
f. _____ Hitting, biting, kicking others.
g. _____ Impoliteness, disrespect.
h. _____ Inconsideration of others' personal property, pets.

You might find it interesting, since no one but you knows what your responses are, to answer questions 1 through 4 twice, once with the answers you know you ought to be putting down and once with the *real* answers. Just the differences between the two sets can suggest your true, deepest feelings about the parental image you present to the world.

In questions 1 through 4, the most image-conscious choices are the first ones, and to a lesser extent, the second. The third response for each question represents low sensitivity to image.

Question 5 requires some thought. Items *b* and *d* are not particularly noticeable to an outside observer. If you ranked them high, you're probably not greatly image-conscious. Items *g* and *h* are not within the capability of a child this age. If you ranked them high, you are expecting far too much of a one-year-old, and your image sensitivity is probably quite high. Items *a, c,* and *f* are very visible; people notice them and disapprove. Did you rank them high? Item *e* is not only a breach of obedience, it is exceedingly dangerous. An inattentive one-year-old (and *all* one-year-olds are inattentive!) could run out in front of a moving car when you called, for example. Ranking that one high indicates concern for the child as well as the image.

One last little exercise: If you saw these behaviors in other people's children, would you rank them differently? Does that different ranking suggest that you expect more of your own child than you do of others? That's an image-conscious indicator.

Investing in an image is almost never good for the

child. Either unrealistic behavior is expected, or the intense pressure to appear good destroys the child's infantile but sincere attempts to actually be good.

Now, when the child is testing and defying, building an identity, image takes the worst beating. Promoting it will increase parental anxiety exponentially. Even worse, promoting it will certainly cost the child happiness, growth, and self-esteem.

The Perfect Versus the Effective Parent

The alternative to perfection is really superior. Work to become an effective parent, and everything else will fall into line. Parents who try to become "good" parents can easily become more concerned about their image as a parent to others than about what is really best for their children. Not only is it ineffective for raising a happy child, it increases parental anxiety. The "effective" parent is going to do whatever it takes to help the child grow, letting the chips and the image fall where they may. In a word, *effectiveness* means child-centered, not self-centered.

The perfectionistic parent is essentially self-centered, worrying "How will I look?" rather than child-centered. And that is the whole difference. Effectiveness is an achievable standard. Effectiveness is *whatever works best*. Effectiveness is flexible. If this doesn't work, let's try that. Effectiveness means matching your parenting techniques and style with the unique temperament of each of your children, adjusting as necessary when your child grows and changes.

It does not mean that Marsha Jasper should be a calm and collected mother like Carrie Parker. It does mean that

Marsha must learn to let go of her perceived need to be a "good" or "perfect" mom.

It does not mean that Jenny needs to devote all her waking hours to Sara's care. It does mean that Jenny must stay on top of her toddler's needs and meet them as best she can.

The best you can do is plenty good enough.

There are other steps you can take to reduce your anxiety while striving for effectiveness rather than perfection. Basically, these come under an umbrella topic of setting realistic goals. We'll let Jenny and Sara illustrate.

Reducing Anxiety

Jenny was going to be late for work. She had to get Sara ready, take her to the sitter down the block, and make it to work at the fast-food restaurant by 6:00 A.M. Why, oh why, did her parents have to be out of town this weekend, when she had the early shift?

She had gotten up in plenty of time. It was Sara who was gumming up the works. Still bleary-eyed with sleep, the baby crabbed and squirmed and fought getting dressed. When Jenny tried to put her shoes on her, she curled her toes up. She spilled grape juice on her T-shirt. Change the shirt. As Jenny headed for the door, Sara pooped in her diaper. It leaked. Change the diaper. Change everything.

Jenny finally got Sara stuffed in her carseat. She still might make it if she hit all the lights right. Gunning it, she backed out of the driveway and slammed on the brakes. She avoided by *inches—inches!*—backing right into a passing van. Sara started howling.

Jenny jumped out of the car, ready to scream at the van, but the other motorist had continued on. Angry, frightened, frustrated to tears, she kicked violently at their freestanding mailbox. The post creaked. She pounded on the roof of her car with both fists as Sara screamed inside. Finally, her initial energy drained, she crossed her arms on the car roof, laid her forehead on them, and simply wept.

"Jenny?"

She snapped erect and wheeled, her nose running.

Old Mrs. Gernrich. The lady always walked her dumb little dog early in the morning. With her ancient cockapoo expressing mild interest in the mailbox post, she stood there smiling. Not laughing at Jenny or smirking. Just smiling.

Jenny babbled a few words of explanation, but they were garbled; she sounded worse than Sara.

"Jenny? Are you doing the best you can?"

"Well, sure, yeah, bu—"

"Then that's plenty good enough." Dragging the cockapoo by its leash, Mrs. Gernrich pulled the back door open. "Grace, down the street, is watching Sara today while you work, right? I'll take her to Grace's. You get on your way." The lady stood erect with the screaming baby locked in a professional wrestling hold of some sort. "If you're late, you're late. Don't take chances with traffic. Be extra careful what you're doing because you're angry right now."

Jenny hesitated only a moment. She handed Mrs. Gernrich the diaper bag and kissed Sara with a quick admonition to be good. Then she kissed Mrs. Gernrich loudly and wetly on the cheek.

Realistic Goals

The best you can do is plenty good enough.

Everybody knows that. It's common sense. But a desire for perfection seems too often to get in the way of common sense.

Are there any perfect parents? One. In heaven. You are not Him. Nor can you ever hope to become the first perfect earthly parent. You've already blown it.

The best you can do is plenty good enough.

Still, perfection floats out there on the horizon, beckoning, as if somehow it were an attainable goal. People whose basic nature tends to perfectionism anyway have a particularly difficult time accepting the inevitability of imperfection. Perfectionism is a subtly attractive compulsion for two almost contradictory reasons. First it gets results—perfectionistic people are doers, the overachievers schools and employers love. But perfectionism can also be attractive because it can keep a person from trying. Most perfectionists are intensely afraid of making mistakes. Thus, some of them won't even try something challenging because it is likely to end in failure. "I can't meet my standards at that so why even bother?" is some perfectionists' mind-set.

"Failure? Oh, I wouldn't exactly call Brian a failure," smirked Tom Jasper. No, but the perfectionist would not be able to accept mistakes the parents make *or* mistakes the small child makes. And there will be plenty of those.

A healthier attitude? The famous screenwriter John Sayles phrased it well. He said, "I run into people all the time who are paralyzed by the fact that they might fail. To me, there is no failure. This is all an exploration."

Paralysis and anxiety. Frustration in an eighteen-month-old who is just trying his or her wings. Because it stymies the exploration of life by making impossible demands, perfectionism and its cousin over-expectation are destructive to children and to parents and to that all-important bonded relationship between them.

Do you have a problem with perfectionism? Hint: True perfectionists rarely think they do. I invite you to try this casual survey. Check the statements that apply to you.

_____ I have difficulty doing something once and leaving it alone. I'll redo a task to get it right.

_____ If my child makes a mistake, it is my responsibility to call the child's attention to it and, if possible, direct the child to correct it.

_____ I dislike a mess. As soon as my child is done coloring or painting, I see that it is immediately picked up.

_____ I frequently remind my child (possibly my spouse as well) to pick up toys and keep the room clean.

_____ If my child gets dirty (other than soiled diapers), I immediately change the child's clothes. I bathe the child daily, or nearly so.

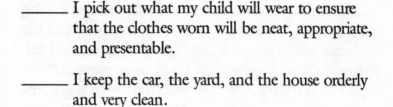

_____ I pick out what my child will wear to ensure that the clothes worn will be neat, appropriate, and presentable.

_____ I keep the car, the yard, and the house orderly and very clean.

If three or more of those statements ring your bell, you ought to consider addressing perfectionistic tendencies as they relate to your parenting. Perfectionism is a compulsion in that it is a behavior that the perfectionist is driven to. You might say the perfectionist has lost the choice to strive or not to strive for perfection.

The saddest part is that this compulsion is easily transmitted to the next generation. The kids will go in one of two directions—either falling into the perfectionist rut or kicking over the traces and leaping to the opposite extreme. You may be providing your children a legacy of anxiety.

What is an alternative? A subtle change in attitude can make all the difference. In any situation when you feel you must correct behavior, appearance, cleanliness, or any other aspect of your baby's world, *Stop!*

Instead of making the correction immediately, pause long enough to ask yourself two points: Is it a problem as it is? Will correcting it send the right message to my child?

It is a problem if it poses a breach of safety for the baby or others (toys scattered on stairs are a hazard; scattered on the living room floor, they are not), a severe breach of hygiene (messy, leaky diaper for example), or some miscellaneous breach (something outside will be ruined if left in the rain).

And what will the message be? "You must always pick up your toys," is not a relevant message to a one-year-old at this level of maturity. Next year, yes. This year, not yet. "Be neat" is not relevant for the same reasons. "You are naughty [to get dirty] [to be careless] [to be clumsy] . . ." Same thing. A kid is a kid.

Correcting a toddler who cannot yet understand or control the behavior that's being corrected tells the child, "You don't measure up, kid." Does that message stick? Absolutely. If you want the child to meet high standards later, the baby is going to have to enjoy a high level of self-esteem. Building now will provide a stronger foundation for success later.

Do you spoil them? Let them get away with murder? Certainly not. But neither ought you to demand super-baby performance. Draw lines, but do not draw them too close to a one-year-old.

How About You?

You've analyzed your tendency toward perfection and your concern about image. Either or both could be making your child's toddlerhood less than it ought to be and robbing you of the pleasure of parenting this special age. I offer you three statements. Can you make them in good conscience? If not, you have just identified an area of your life that needs work.

My kid comes first. Regardless of what the neighbors think or what the appearance may be, I will work for the goal of a happy, growing baby and not the false goal of *the appearance* of a happy, growing baby.

The best I can do is plenty good enough. I promise myself I will actively resist perfectionist tendencies when they crop up. I cannot achieve perfection, my child is not perfect, and from this time on we will work with what we have instead of what I wish my child were.

Relationships always come first.

The antidotes to perfectionism and image-consciousness lie in the statements themselves. The more you keep them in mind, the more you remind yourself of them. The more you apply them to the many daily incidents they can influence, the more they will shape your attitudes. Let them. Your baby's happiness is worth any effort you can make.

Perfectionism and image-consciousness are not the only causes for parental anxiety by any means. Sometimes, a child simply presents an insurmountable challenge. The parents' hearts are set on a better outcome than will be possible.

Parenting a Difficult Child

Sara was shaping into a difficult child. She came unglued easily and frequently when things didn't go her way. She butted heads a lot with Grandma and sometimes with others. Her steps of separation and individuation were shaky and fraught with friction.

The difficult child is the one in the family who has

been the hardest to raise, has caused the most stress and conflict in the family, has the most difficulty making and keeping friends, and typically will have the most problems in school.

One of the roots of difficulty is simple spoilage. The entitled child is always difficult, the exempt child infinitely more so. Once the windows have closed on entitlement and exemption, after about age three, the two conditions are almost impossible to reverse.

Another root of problems is attention deficit disorder (ADD). Here, the difficult child is not trying to be difficult. Rather, the child is marching to a drummer no one else hears. ADD cannot be diagnosed in a child this young. I don't suggest that. But I want you to attune yourself to the possibility that when you encounter difficult behavior you will realize that the difficulty may not be the child's intent at all. There are many reasons a child may be difficult without meaning to be. Eventually, Jenny would learn that ADD was Sara's problem.

She, like other ADD kids, stands on a curious cusp: at high risk for either prison or greatness. Winston Churchill possessed a learning disability similar to ADD. A lot of criminals do.

Parents of these children are going to suffer considerable anxiety under any circumstance. Where they spend their energies will play a large part in determining the outcome. When parents struggle under the expectation that things will change with this difficult child—things will get easier the more the parents work—they are doomed to failure. Things will not change. In contrast, the parents who accept that their child needs different strategies for meeting life will see some degree of success—sometimes a very high degree.

The bottom line is that you will have to know and understand your child as he or she is, and work with the difference rather than try to change it.

Handling Guilt

When the outcome is less than perfect or even seems to be shaping up that way, parents somehow manage to see what they should have done, whether what they see is actually valid or not. *If only I* . . . creeps in. Guilt can cause intense anxiety.

"If only I had stayed in Brooklyn and had never come near this forsaken rabbit run." Once Walt Raines got started grousing about his son Brendan and about Texas, he couldn't quit. He had moved with his family from New York to Irving, Texas, four years ago. He had not yet adjusted to the different surroundings and lifestyle.

"Ceci thinks Brendan will turn out fine. We should live so long. He's over the top already. You should see him try to blow his pierced nose with all that hardware in it."

Actually, I *had* seen that. Walt and his wife, Ceci, had brought their son, Brendan, to me, asking for help. When Brendan broke down in tears on his second visit, he went through a dozen tissues. Then he confided, "The stud and the gold safety pin? They're a pain in the nose. I mean it. I'd take 'em out in a minute, but then Dad would think he won, and I'm not going to let him have that."

Walt continued his tirade. "Back on Hagerthy Street

while Brendan was growing up, the older kids on the block would be raising Cain. The lady next door, Mrs. Goldfein, she was always saying, 'Oy, the neighborhood.' The kids there were wild. But not Brendan. He came home like he was s'posed to—you know what I'm saying?"

And then the tough, pragmatic Walt Raines broke down also. "I know I shoulda been more a father to Brendan. The girl, she was easy to raise. Just turn her loose with her mama. But Brendan. I guess I should be content he's not—you know, one of those. But if I'd only been more a father."

He pronounced it *fodder*. His New York accent might have been out of place, but his heart was right, and so was his desire to change the fabric of his family somehow. "I'm the fodder figure, right? So what I say goes. And I should say, 'All right, youse guys, we're gonna be a real family,' and it should happen, right? Only I know it ain't gonna, and that makes me sadder than ever."

"How about your relationship with Ceci?"

He shrugged generously. "What's to complain? I don't mess around none and she don't mess around none, so we're solid." A pause. " 'Course, I can't say I been the best for her. Oh, sure, I provide well. Good provider. But . . ."

"But?"

"Aaggh." It was partly a growl, partly a clearing of the throat. "So many things I'd do different if we could do 'em over, know what I'm saying? So many things."

His guilt quotient, so to speak, was very high. How about yours? If you can list six things right now, rapidly, off the top of your head, that you would do differently if you could (not just about child raising but about life in general) you may be carrying a burden of guilt so heavy it increases your parental anxiety, as it did Walt Raines's.

Guilt itself is bad enough, but it usually spurs resentment—whether that resentment is toward another person presumed responsible (a spouse, a boss, a sibling), toward circumstances, or toward a job or situation. Anger of that sort always rubs off onto children, even extremely small children.

Self-talk can help. For each *If only* . . . you think of, apply these three points step by step:

1. What specific situation has my action/inaction caused? Could it be worse? Could some other action/inaction on my part have caused a worse result? A better one? What did I do *right* in regard to the situation?

Walt Raines believed that his shortcomings as a father could have led his son to homosexuality and was glad that was not the case. Whether such assumptions are correct or incorrect is not at issue. Guilt is a matter of feelings as much as of fact. He expressed strong feelings, and it was the feelings that had to be resolved.

In your explorations of these questions, look not for the cold facts so much as for your innermost feelings. Wrong assumptions can cause as much trouble as correct ones.

2. Have I asked God's forgiveness for my shortcoming? If not, I shall do so right now. I accept that He forgives freely and that I must forgive myself. I do so.

3. It's done. It's over. Only today and tomorrow remain. What positive steps am I going to take *now* to allay the situation I believe my action or inaction caused?

God's forgiveness is literally the perfect answer to guilt.

If you need help claiming that solution, discuss it with a trusted friend, adviser, or pastor.

A contributory cause of guilt feelings and parental anxiety that I see repeatedly, every day, is a powerful one: working parents.

The Working Parent

As she juggles childcare with school and, later, with making a living, Jenny Lawton represents what millions of men and women must contend with daily. "How can I be a good parent when I'm out of the house from eight to twelve hours a day?"

People who are not caught in that bind have a hard time understanding how these working parents feel. They say, "I don't have much sympathy. If they would settle for a somewhat lower standard of living, one of them could stay home with the child." Usually this mind-set is accompanied by, "Now when *I* was raising toddlers . . ."

Today's economic climate is not that simple or rosy. Most households need two paychecks just to maintain the home and get the older children through school. I'm talking about grade school and high school; college is a whole 'nother ball game. If the parent ends up single for one reason or another, working is an absolute necessity. There are more resources for the widowed than for the divorced, but rarely can the single parent of a toddler enjoy the luxury of staying home. What fertile ground for anxiety!

Ah, but there are options for both lifestyle and day care. Let's look at them from the viewpoint of a toddler's best interests. And because single parenting presents unique problems, I will address that separately, to follow.

Remember that the toddler needs, above all things, attachment. The child's later social development, from enduring friendships to solid marriage—I am not overstating this—depends upon attachment right now, during toddlerhood. A strong personal relationship with the primary caregiver is essential and should be the goal of any day care situation.

One Parent Stays Home

Tom Jasper and Marsha represent by far the best option. One parent stays home with the child during these crucial first three years. To achieve that, would you have to adopt a lower standard of living? It might be worth it in the long run. Remember that a small child thinks nothing of material surroundings or status or the kind of automobile the family drives—none of that. That's grown-up stuff. If you can put it aside until the child is in school and thereby provide the child with a stay-at-home parent, by all means do so.

Which parent works and which stays home? It doesn't matter. Young friends of mine, the Bruces, met and married in grad school. Both earned their doctorates. When the baby arrived, about the same time as the Ph.D.s, they decided, "Whoever gets the best offer goes to work. Post-docs don't count." She was the first to receive an invitation to a position as a teaching professor, and it pays well. He stays home with the baby.

Does Daddy as primary caregiver work satisfactorily? Beautifully!

When Walt Raines said, "I know I shoulda been more a father to Brendan. The girl, she was easy to raise. Just turn her loose with her mama," I winced. It's a common viewpoint of most fathers, but it does not serve the child well.

Invariably, a daughter's opinion of herself—her self-esteem, if you will—will reflect her father's opinion of her—her mother's opinion secondarily, but her father's primarily. When Daddy takes an active part in his girl's life during these crucial first three years, the benefits extend a lifetime.

Alternate Work Schedules

Two of our psychotherapists here at the Minirth Meier New Life Clinic, husband and wife, are raising their family in just this way. It is not a case of two part-time workers. Both work nearly full time. But they have successfully juggled their schedules so that one or the other is home. One day a week they put their one-year-old and three-year-old into day care and both work.

If your job permits that kind of flexibility, it's a splendid way to go. My coworkers' children, a girl and a boy, know both parents intimately. Object constancy is served when the parents leave and then faithfully return. And both parents are advancing their careers. It's the best for everyone involved.

Work in Part at Home

This is not so rosy an option as it first seems. "I work at home," a contract editor told me. She accepts freelance editing assignments from two publishing houses, line editing book manuscripts. Line editing requires concentration; you are looking not at the content but at the spelling, punctuation, capitalization, and all.

"The kids were really distracting. They needed this. They needed that. They're one and three, so you know how that is. I couldn't work five minutes without an interruption. It wasn't the kids' fault. They really did need this and that."

She solved that dilemma by hiring a neighbor to come into her home to serve the children's needs while she worked. This arrangement was much superior to day care and less expensive, but she had a hard time getting past the guilt that she couldn't handle it all herself.

With the fax machine, computer, enhanced phone services, and a more relaxed attitude on the part of upper management, home offices are becoming practical. There was the day when, if you weren't sitting at a desk under the boss's nose, you weren't working. Fortunately, at least for jobs that do not depend upon that requirement, smart companies are relaxing it. Not only does working at least part of the time at home make good ecological sense, reducing pollution and congestion, it also makes good family sense.

Housekeeper/Nanny

You protest, "By the time you pay a housekeeper, you might as well dump one salary and leave a parent at home."

When both parents are making good money and advancing the careers of both is an important consideration, this is a good option. The toddler remains in a familiar environment with a single primary caregiver. No, it is not as good as having Mommy or Daddy being constantly at hand, but it works, assuming the opportunity for healthy attachment is there.

The caveat with such an arrangement is that the face who arrives each day should be the same face. Find one dependable person, not a parade of people to whom the child is not closely attached.

Kibbutz

In this country, the communal work unit is not a normal option. For many years now, however, Israel has not only been using the kibbutz but also studying its long-term effects. Children raised communally in a nursery with many (usually older) people in attendance do surprisingly well. They seem at ease socially, particularly with their elders, a grace that our children sometimes lack.

Day Care

What a fount of parental anxiety is day care! Frankly, the anxiety is justified to an extent. Day care, by which I mean a business enterprise in a private home or a nursery, is a poor substitute for the presence of a parent or constant primary caregiver such as Jenny's mom. Day care does have its pluses, however. It encourages self-reliance—that is, independence, and to a degree, greater self-confidence.

However, a child younger than one year old needs constancy from caretakers and will reap no benefit whatever from a day care setting, particularly if the parent(s) is absent for more than three or four hours at a stretch. The predictable presence of parents helps solidify the infant's emerging sense of self. Short stays with a trusted baby-sitter allow the infant to learn that parents can be trusted to return—and allows the parents a long-awaited break!

The toddler needs the strong personal bond just as

much as the infant does, for the toddler is stepping out into a wild and hairy unknown world and desperately needs the comforting backup that strongly attached parents provide.

"But I have no choice!" Many, many parents must of necessity say that. So, of the day care options, what forms of care are best? In order of preference:

1. Single-person care (preferably by a relative or caring adult).

This is best by far. Jenny Lawton was blessed with a mother willing to take Sara when Jenny was at school or work. This situation was almost as good as if Mommy stayed home. Not *as* good, but almost. Note that it is the same caregiver day after day. That's important; in order to learn trust, the child needs to bond into a solid, constant relationship, and that won't happen with a random sequence of baby-sitters.

2. Small-group day care in a private home with no more than three other children and the same concerned adult in attendance each day.

Almost as good. The caregiver may well employ an assistant. That's fine, so long as a continual close relationship is possible with one person.

3. Day care with a good adult-to-child ratio.

So-so. What's a good ratio? An adult for every three or four kids. If the facility specializes in under-threes, the ratio should be one adult for two or three children. Be forewarned. Few day care facilities catering to the diaper crowd boast a ratio that good. Some states step in and legislate ratios. Know what your state laws require and be certain the facility you choose observes them.

Again, look for those hard-to-describe qualities that allow your child to become strongly attached to a caring adult.

4. Inconsistent care.

To be avoided. In some facilities, particularly larger ones, the childcare is at best custodial. The motto seems to be, "Keep a lid on the little varmints until Mommy or Daddy writes a check and take them away." The saddest situations feature a large number of children and a small number of adults, with frequent staff turnovers.

In fact, heed turnover rate at any facility you investigate. A high number of caregivers hiring on and then leaving suggests that the pay is poor, the working conditions are bad, or some other problem haunts the place. You do not want to leave your toddler in the care of a worker with a low incentive to go the extra mile. Toddlers need that extra mile.

Remember that at this age in particular your kid is no picnic in the park. The toddler needs to identify with one caring adult and to test limits in a safe, consistent, loving environment. A toddler's testing and individuation can try the patience of Job. The caregiver must be able to understand what is happening and help your child.

How long is okay, and how long is too long for a child to be ensconced in day care? My recommendation: minimal. Whatever you can do to minimize the number of hours the child is separated from the parents will help immensely. There are no guidelines, for some children accept day care more comfortably than do others. Some never really accept it at all. I would like to think that a child under age two would be in custodial care outside the home for four hours or less per day.

What, though, is the greatest single source of parental anxiety? Single parenting.

The Special Case of the Single Parent

Ruth and her two teen daughters, Shauna and her little Afton, Jenny and Sara—single parents come in all flavors. All have the same problem, that of raising a child without a spouse, and all suffer incredible guilt in addition to anxiety.

Until recently, the prevailing opinion in America went as follows: Children are better off in a single-parent home than in a two-parent home torn by constant friction and fighting. Also, the younger a child is when the split occurs, the easier it will be for that child to accept. Children will get over the pain of divorce in a year or two.

Then, long-term studies of the children of divorce brought some cold data to light. Over a period of five, ten, and twenty years, children of divorce in the studies have had constant difficulty building deep relationships. They also earn less money than do adult children from two-parent homes, get into more financial problems, stand a statistically higher risk of substance abuse . . . the list goes on.

There's no way around it; very small children in a one-parent situation often cannot receive the kinds of nurturing required for them to learn how to build deep relationships. Parental anxiety and guilt, already incredibly high among singles, just rocketed out of sight.

Guilt. Frustration. Because their child is not growing up with both a father and mother, most single parents try to be both, believing *I should be able to pull this off. I have to be able to pull this off.* But they can't because it is impossible. Guilt and frustration multiply.

Let us assume from this point that you are a single parent. Those of you who are not, I ask that you do not skip this section. You have friends in this situation and certainly a number of singles in your church. They need help, and if you want to help them effectively, you must know their options and circumstances. So please read on.

You, the single parent, have a variety of possible options in regard to lifestyle, attitude, and day care. We have examined day care. What works for two parents also works for one. Let's look at the other categories from the viewpoint of a toddler's needs. In this, I am assuming there are no older children. Older children complicate the picture considerably and present unique challenges that cannot be addressed with generalities.

Attitudes

"If your sweater fell in the lake it'd cause an environmental disaster. Aren't you going to wash it soon?" Jenny's mom scowled with disdain at Jenny's very most ultimate favorite garment.

"You never did like this sweater, did you? Yeah, I'll drop it off at the cleaner's." Jenny carried her precious sweater out to the laundry room so her mom wouldn't have to look at it. *She's always on me for something. With sarcasm. I don't know which I hate worse, the constant picking or the sarcasm.*

She emptied the sweater's two patch pockets on top of the dryer. Here was Shauna Moore's phone number. Shauna Moore. The woman she'd met in the pediatrician's office. She tossed the paper in the wastebasket, sorted through the sticks of gum for the stuff that was still good, puzzled a few moments wondering where the rubber O-ring had come from, and looked at that paper down there in the wastebasket. She fished it out and stuffed it in her jeans pocket. The next day, she called it.

That afternoon, Shauna and Jenny took their two daughters to the park. Why did Jenny do this? She didn't know what to say. Shauna seemed so much older, so much more mature and worldly wise. While Sara and Afton played on the junior-size jungle gym, Jenny and Shauna shared a bag of fresh-roasted peanuts.

Shauna was the one who leaped beyond the casual pleasantries they had opened with. "So how's your guilt coming?"

"How'd you know I have some?" *What a stupid thing to say, you dumb enchilada! She knows because she's in the same boat. She knows everything you think and feel.* Jenny shelled a warm peanut. "Okay, I guess. Do you ever get over it?"

"Nope. You can't imagine how guilty I felt 'cause Afton doesn't have a daddy. He offered to marry me. He even tried to force me to. I had to get a restraining order and then I just up and moved."

"Why work so hard to avoid it if you feel guilty?"

"He's abusive. I didn't realize it when I started going

with him. Or maybe I just didn't want to see it. I don't know. I was really crazy about him. Then when I found out I was pregnant I started looking at him pretty hard and close. He swore he'd change, but I was afraid to believe him."

"Regret it?"

"Sometimes, when the money's real tight. But no." Shauna grinned. "I got over it by volunteering as a housemaid at a battered women's shelter. Cured me in a hurry. I'd much rather be working for them than knocking on their door with a black eye and a scared baby. Or worse, a battered baby."

Jenny pondered Shauna's choices against her own. Her choices didn't seem as clear. Darren wasn't abusive. He was just—well, a big zero. Not interested, not there for her, and certainly not in the throes of love. Or even in the throes of like, particularly.

Shauna continued, "Anyway, I decided I'd make the best decisions I could, and I assumed I'd make some of them wrong—not trying to, of course, it's just the way it is—and go with the flow. Know what I mean?"

"Yeah, pretty much." *Go with the flow.* Was Jenny drifting along too much with the flow, or was it a God-given way for her to survive with her decision to keep Sara? She wished life were closer to black and white instead of all these shades of gray.

Attitudes. Jenny was doing well to examine hers. And she had already taken a major step in adopting one of the attitudes any single parent must adopt in order to succeed—asking for help.

1. A single parent must adopt an attitude of asking for and accepting help.

Jenny Lawton found it extremely difficult to ask for help. In fact, when she called Shauna, she did not let herself consciously recognize that as a request for help.

Friends? None of her high school friends could relate to her situation, and they didn't seem interested in maintaining close contact. They were bustling through their own lives on a greatly divergent track from hers.

She certainly felt uncomfortable going to other, invariably older, members of her church. Did she feel a judgmental undercurrent? Rejection? Quite probably. Christ's soldiers comprise the only army in the world that shoots its wounded.

That left, so far as she knew, her parents. They had a duty to help (though not all parents see it that way). In Jenny's case, they were the best choice at the time as she finished school and got started in the world. However:

2. A single parent must be the parent.

Jenny was not. She had the name but not the game. Because she was the child in her own parent-child relationship with Mom and Dad, she abrogated parenting Sara by default. Her mom served as mother to both her and Sara.

It always works out that way.

Were Jenny aware of this dynamic, could she change it? No.

A friend of mine we'll call Sandy described why. "I hate flying down to Phoenix to visit my widowed mom. Three days with her, four days max; then I either have to leave or go nuts. Picture this. I'm fifty-two years old, all right? I walk in, we talk, everything's great. I'm on vacation, so I'm going to kick back and relax. I break out a bag of tortilla chips. It's four o'clock. Mom tells me not to eat any because I'll spoil my appetite for dinner. She doesn't want me to go out in the rain; I might catch cold. I'm supposed to put on a sweater when I go outside because it's only sixty-five degrees, Phoenix's low. But that's still twenty degrees warmer than the high I just came out of to visit her. Three days of that drives you right out of your tree, no matter how good your intentions when you first get there."

Parents are ever parents, which makes their children ever children. The older parents get, the more they cling to the role. An elderly parent will probably have more trouble abstaining from the sort of behavior Sandy described than will a younger one. Still, the role is too ingrained to reverse.

There are only two really good solutions. One is to talk it out with the parents, set up guidelines, and write them down. This requires an uncommonly high level of communication. The parents have to desire to adhere to them, and that rarely happens. The second solution is to limit contact. Move out. Build a life outside the direct intervention of the parents.

Almost invariably, too, another flip-flop occurs in parent-child relationships, this one between the little one and any parent not well wed to his or her spouse. By definition, the single parent qualifies as being not well wed. The little one becomes, in subtle ways, a surrogate companion and confidant to this parent.

The technical term for this is *emotional incest*. It is not incestuous in a sexual context, although at an extreme, it could conceivably become so. Think of it as an energy transfer. The parent pours the energy of nurturing into the child, and with that energy the child grows emotionally and psychologically. When the parent calls upon the child for nurturing, however, the energy flow reverses. This drains the child in a hurry (for the child has almost no such energy in reserve), crippling the child's emotional and psychological growth.

Emotional incest almost invariably occurs to some extent in a single parent's situation. You can't prevent it, but you can minimize it by minimizing its causes and monitoring your attitude and habits continually.

The causes are complex, but basically, the problem arises because single parents become isolated from the rest of the world. The rest of the world sympathizes with a widowed parent, although it tends to back off, nervous and uncertain. But divorced and unwed parents receive almost no sympathy.

Another cause of isolation is the tyranny of time. Single parents have to squeeze into one day what it takes two parents to achieve—job, nurturing, and possibly courting. There is simply no time to foster a variety of outside relationships to fill emotional needs.

Thus isolated, the single parent becomes enmeshed in the only other really close human being available, the child. To quote Shauna, "For a while there, until I broke free, the universe closed down until only Afton and I were in it."

In what ways specifically might a parent inadvertently reverse the nurturing role?

• *Calling upon the child to take on tasks, responsibilities, and decisions the child is not ready to handle, no matter how pseudo-mature the child may seem.* This is important for an older child. For example, a ten-year-old has no business undertaking a responsibility such as childcare for younger siblings or household maintenance that requires adult stability and knowledge should an emergency crop up.

This principle is also important to a tiny child. A toddler should be given no real responsibility yet for his or her own actions. The child's attention span and knowledge of the world are not yet adequate. Leaving a child unattended for even a moment is one such instance. Another would be expecting the child to remain within the confines of an unfenced, unmarked area such as an open yard. Certainly the child understands not to stray, but distractions and forgetfulness rule at this age.

• *Using the child as a confidant, companion, or surrogate emotional spouse.* This is especially invidious when the child is older. "I don't know," the single dad might ask his thirteen-year-old child. "Should I date this woman I just met?"

No, no, no! Children, in their inexperience, cannot advise or validate the parent's emotional quandaries. One would not expect that sort of thing of a toddler, but the emotionally dependent parent may make similar impositions. Consider these comments made to a toddler:

"You're my little man."

"It's just you and me."

"You know better than that. [Mommy or Daddy] is depending on you."

Children certainly love the feeling of being considered

as little adults. But the energy drains them rather than replenishes their reserves.

• *Expecting the child to make the parent happy.* Never is this the child's role. When the child does so simply by being a child, wonderful! But it must not be an expectation.

Ruth and her two daughters illustrate the problem. Without realizing it, Ruth nurtured a fantasy that her two perfect daughters, reared without being denied anything, would feel so grateful toward her that they would always be there for her. But Sherry and Susan were spoiled, and spoiled children are never grateful. Was this fantasy unrealistic? Of course. But not to Ruth.

Were Jenny to examine her deepest motives, she'd find this expectation within herself as well. Somehow, Sara would complete a certain unhappiness within Jenny.

Ruth devoted her life to Sherry and Susan. She did not date, and she possessed few friends. And even though she had a part-time job, most of her energy and free time went into making Sherry and Susan happy. So who met Ruth's needs for companionship, emotional exchange, emotional intimacy—the needs of every human being?

With no peers handy she had to turn to her daughters, however unconsciously. Rest assured that human beings will get their needs met, no matter what.

When Ruth's daughters failed to complete her fantasy, she lost what little input they had provided toward her emotional needs. Ruth had sown the seeds in their toddlerhood; now she was left empty.

Is emotional incest abusive? It certainly is, because it imposes upon the child a task that the child is not equipped to handle. More important, it drains away the energy necessary to grow. Now, right here at toddler stage, is the time to build a defense against it.

Because it occurs universally, Jenny, too, would have to counteract this constant tendency toward emotional incest by being aware of its insidious progress and resisting it. It begins to occur when the child is an infant and by now, toddlerhood, the parent may well be drawing a great deal of emotional energy from this little tyke who needs the adult so much. Being the most important person in someone else's world is a powerful emotional boost. So are the baby smiles and baby hugs. Even at this time, when the child is a little more than a year old, a complete change of attitude is necessary.

To minimize this tendency, single parents must monitor their own behavior and feelings, watching for signs that they are letting the child be the parent. In addition, they should have at least one other close friend, a same-sex peer, for support. In Jenny's case, that person could very well be Shauna Moore. They should also cultivate a fairly wide variety of other friends—six good ones at a minimum—from which to draw support, companionship, advice, comfort, and sometimes simple logistics, swapping baby-sitting, for example, or sharing rides.

The single parent who is able to ask for and receive help from a variety of sources will not be as likely to look to the child to fulfill the parent's emotional needs.

3. Single parents must come to grips with the fact that they are partnerless.

Ruth, Shauna, and Jenny, each in their unique situations, owed it to their kids to accept the fact that they were going to be doing this alone. Should help materialize, fine. Happy surprise. But that's only a possibility. The present situation, being partnerless, is the reality.

Ruth grieved her divorce and the stigma it placed upon her but not the actual loss of Rick's participation. If you have a loss in your life, you must grieve both it and the secondary results of that loss.

Jenny did not feel a need to grieve Darren's absence from her life. She found herself strangely unattached to him at an emotional level. Like Ruth, she did, however, need to grieve the loss of Darren's participation.

Shauna had completed this phase well.

4. Single parents must face reality squarely.

Messing with reality, either for yourself or your child, is no way to find emotional health. How would Jenny, Ruth, and Shauna handle that point?

• *Single parents shouldn't try to change facts.* Should little Sara and Afton know the truth about their respective fathers? Yes. All at once? Not necessarily. Afton would not be sophisticated enough to comprehend the abusive nature of her father. Sara would not grasp that sometimes a daddy just never gets involved.

• *Single parents should be judicious with facts.* Shauna would be wise to reserve editorial comment about Afton's father both now and in the future—in short, not bad-mouthing him. Telling Afton what a jerk he was would avail little. Warning Afton against going anywhere with a strange man, however, would be essential. I am not suggesting the single parent should compromise the child's safety or happiness by hiding facts. Be circumspect. But also be wise.

Keep in mind that the relationship between the biological father (in Afton's case) and the child is the sole responsibility of the father. Not the mother. Not Shauna. The reverse is equally true, of course. It is not the single parent's job to either build or destroy the child's relationship with the other parent. That is the other parent's responsibility.

Frankly, Ruth blew it in this department. She let the girls know in full detail what she thought of their emotionally detached father. Below conscious level, she was trying to make them despise him as she had come to despise him. The opposite occurred. They turned to him, partly out of fascination (the forbidden too often looks good), partly to spite their mother, and partly to gain favors such as gifts and money that Mom couldn't bestow.

• *Single parents can't be both parents.* A toddler needs both a male and a female parent, comparing, and weighing Every Man and Every Woman against all the people the child will one day encounter. In the next year or two, that need will increase as the child comes to terms with what is called the Oedipus complex.

One parent cannot meet that sort of need, now or later. Period. Second best, and a second-best answer is better than none at all, is to expose the toddler to a good opposite-sex model. Here is where the church must be willing to step forth and help. Combining the first point—that singles must ask for help—with this warning that single parents can't be both parents will provide the toddler with the appropriate answer to a serious need, a way to learn about both genders. Where better than the church can singles find good, God-fearing, opposite-sex models?

The singles and the church must also remember this fifth point:

5. God loves and takes care of single parents too.

Certainly a two-parent family is best. Certainly God ordained marriage and family. But some of Scripture's most important stories deal with single-parent households. The widow of Zarephath, Timothy's upbringing, and James's concern for the fatherless all illustrate that it is indeed possible in God's eyes to do it alone.

6. Single parents must see themselves as having something to give back to society.

Shauna explained it this way: "The attitude I got from the church was, 'You're less fortunate, so we'll help you like we're supposed to help all less-fortunates. We're better than you because we're raising our kids with two parents, the right way, but okay, we'll help you.' They never said it out loud. That was the feeling you got."

Few, indeed, are the churches that manage to push past this undercurrent. It can be reduced in two ways. One way is for singles, if they feel it, to bring it into the open. "This is the unspoken message I'm getting."

The other way is to take off the victim-and-martyr mask the church assumes of you and take an active part in the ministry. Single parents' attitudes can move from the mind-set of feeling needy to the mind-set of feeling needed. It makes all the difference.

Said Shauna, "I started working in the church nursery

a couple of Sundays a month. You know; it was something I could do. Then the pastor asked for volunteers to set up the vacation Bible school. I didn't have the time to do that, between Afton and working on her hearing problems and my job and all. But I could make posters and the flannel-board stuff they needed. They asked for help with costumes for some skits too. I could do that. Finding a Smokey Bear hat was a challenge. And fun. That style is called a campaign hat, did you know that? And they needed a live goat. A live goat, for crying out loud! Did you know there's a national organization of goat farmers? There's gotta be a national organization for just about every single thing in the whole world!"

Jenny watched Shauna's eyes dance as she told about her service. Jenny hadn't felt that enthusiastic about something for a year. More than a year. She yearned for an attitude as upbeat and positive as Shauna's, and she saw now how she could get it.

But then a dismal thought struck her. "You talk about feeling like you're not a victim anymore."

"Or a martyr, right? It's easy to slip into that."

"Yeah. But my mom, she sort of shoves me into it. She lets me know that my life—and hers—are all messed up because of Sara. That's martyr stuff, right?"

Shauna nodded. "It was a big sacrifice financially, but I had to move out. My mama could sure pour on the guilt. And the 'poor me' routine. Like I was getting ready to go out on a date—the first social thing I'd done in six months—and she said, 'You're not going to leave Afton alone again are you? You're away from her all day as it is.'"

Jenny nodded. "I haven't even tried to go out with other people. I don't mean just a guy. I mean anyone."

"Right. So then I moved in with my sister. But I'm looking to change that too. Anyway the best thing I've done lately is get this support group going at church. It's a bunch of parents that get together weekly and just talk about problems. I'm the only single parent so far, but I think a newly divorced father is joining." She stood up and stretched. "It sure is good to get out of the house."

Jenny realized with amazement that it had never occurred to her before that she might live apart from her parents. But why not? She was out of school. Working. Sure, Mom was a big help and a good baby-sitter, but there was that constant undercurrent of friction. Mom pushing the martyrdom thing. Mom taking over Sara's life completely with Jenny, the actual mother, playing the baby-sitter-after-work role. Jenny had other options as well:

• *Living with parents or relatives.* This, Jenny's current option, offered several advantages and disadvantages you should think about if you're parenting a toddler.

The toddler enjoyed the stability of one sitter, one parent, one situation, day in and day out. Children are conservative little creatures who want things to stay the same; they thrive on routine.

On the other hand, if Jenny wanted her own mind-set to move beyond feeling like a victim, she, like Shauna, might have to get away from home to do it.

What is your situation? What are the unspoken feelings in your current household?

Jenny and Sara, ideally, would each have a separate

room. Jenny needed a way to get away from Sara once in a while, to have a life apart. Second best would be one large room with a screen to divide off the nursery.

• *Living in a communal arrangement of people in similar situations.* "There's this house over by the university," said Shauna, "that used to be a fraternity house. Four single-parent families live there. Common kitchen privileges, you take turns cleaning up the living room, and each family gets two or three dorm-style rooms to live in. The activity room is the nursery, and they go in together to pay a permanent, full-time baby-sitter. It's a great arrangement, but it's awfully far from work. I don't know if I'll move there or not."

A friend of Shauna's organized the group of single parents when the frat house went up for sale. An arrangement of that sort can be a blessing for two or more families who want to share housing, childcare, and responsibilities. Before setting up a similar situation of your own, check into zoning restrictions. There are often limits on the number of families permitted to live in any particular unit or neighborhood.

A communal situation of that sort is excellent for the toddler of a single parent, particularly if the group includes both male and female parents. This may well take care of the necessary opposite-sex role model. Assuming the day care arrangement is stable, with one person to whom the child can attach, it will provide an extended-family atmosphere that living alone cannot.

• *Living alone.* "That's what I'd love to do," Jenny confided, "be on my own. My own boss. Yeah!"

It's the dream of nearly every parent. It is also the

most difficult logistically. Besides the obvious problems of finding day care and time enough to maintain the household, the child, and a job, living alone further isolates the parent. That's a problem under any circumstance; this circumstance exacerbates it.

Whatever your situation, weigh it against the measure of what is best for the child. That will be:

1. Stability
2. Ability to bond long-term with a primary caregiver
3. Room to grow, explore, and develop
4. A positive, upbeat attitude on your part, with reduced guilt feelings, and . . .
5. An aggressive desire in you to be an effective parent

6. THE BEGINNING OF THE FUTURE

DISCIPLINE

Chasten your son while there
is hope,
And do not set your heart on
his destruction.

PROVERBS 19:18

When the little tyke toddled into the church nursery for the first time, Shauna and two other attendants said simultaneously, "What a cherub!" He was a bit on the small side for eighteen months, with a delicately chiseled little face, deep-set eyes, and gleaming blond hair.

He cried when his mother left; the silver tears made his long, dark lashes seem even longer. Shauna hugged him, but he shoved away angrily, so she set him down. Quickly he surveyed the room, the toys scattered about, and the eight other toddlers. Then he marched stiff-legged to a small wooden truck, picked it up, and deftly fired it ten feet across the room.

Shauna grabbed his arms and said firmly, "We never throw things in here, Kevin. No more throwing."

He responded by flinging a block, corking Afton in the ear eight feet away.

The nursery manager, Mrs. Foran, scooped him up and trundled him off to the corner, explaining the rules, as Shauna comforted Afton.

Kicking and squalling, Kevin finally wormed down off

the manager's lap. Within thirty seconds he made an earnest effort to brain little Jason with a rubber doll. Only Shauna's flying intervention snatched the doll in time.

As Kevin writhed, screaming, under her arm, Shauna stood erect and looked at Mrs. Foran. "I always wanted to know a celebrity personally. When they send this joker to the chair for serial murder, we'll be able to say, 'We knew him when.'"

Controlling a One-Year-Old

Kevin's parents did not own pets.

On purpose.

"Kevin tends to be a little rough sometimes." That's what Kevin's mom said when he was clawed by their cat, an affable old Siamese who normally never hurt a soul. They found a new home for the cat. This was just after he was mouthed by a neighbor's ten-year-old Labrador retriever reputed to be very good with children. Actually, the Lab *was* very good with kids; she was justified in removing the kid's arm, but she didn't even break the skin.

A child between the ages of one and two rarely poses a threat to adults, so Kevin's parents didn't think much of his aggressive streak. But it came through loud and clear in any day care or nursery situation. The parents considered it a personality trait rather than a serious problem to be resolved. Either they didn't notice or they refused to admit that none of their friends wanted Kevin to come over and play with their children.

Kevin's parents did not believe in corporal punishment. When they corrected his behavior, they explained to him why they were doing so. They tried to meet his every demand, understanding that infants instinctively know what they need.

All this came out after church when Mrs. Foran asked the parents to discuss his behavior for a few minutes. "I'll be blunt, Mr. and Mrs. York. Your son has strong antisocial tendencies that must be addressed."

"Oh?" Mrs. York's eyes narrowed the least bit. "Are you a psychologist, Mrs. Foran?"

"If my fifty years' experience working with kids doesn't impress you, find yourself a good psychologist. But do take steps to reverse this now, while it's reversible."

That was when Mrs. York went into detail to defend her disciplining strategies. Then she quizzed Mrs. Foran closely, making certain that no one in the nursery had inflicted corporal punishment upon poor little Kevin. She seemed somewhat suspicious that maybe Mrs. Foran was less than truthful when she said, "No, we didn't."

And Shauna added to herself, *But it sure crossed our minds.*

The nursery manager concluded, "Your discipline strategies aren't working on Kevin, and the situation is going to get nothing but worse as he grows older and bigger and more sly and sophisticated. He's supposed to be learning important lessons just now about what is right and wrong. Make sure he gets them, in no uncertain terms."

Mrs. York stiffened. "You certainly aren't suggesting I strike him."

"Whatever works, ma'am. Whatever works."

Choosing a Strategy

If one way of doing it worked for every child, discipline would be so much simpler. If children this age were not making their first attempts at individuation, discipline would be so much simpler. If parents relied more on their observations, really studying their little ones, discipline would be so much simpler.

Let's look at strategy choices that will provide a maximal desired effect, a child who is finding a personal identity and preparing for the next great step, *self*-discipline. Those strategies will vary according to whether you are working with a fairly difficult child like Sara, an "easy" child like Brian, a child just entering this age group, a child like Kevin who is already entitled and must be turned around, or a fifteen-year-old such as the beleaguered Brendan Raines and his dad.

In all these cases, discipline will not be simple.

Discipline in the Past—Last Year

Before one year of age, everything a child knows about right and wrong comes from outside. *Wrong* is whatever Mommy and Daddy forbid. *Wrong* is pulling parts off stuffed toys, dolls, or the cat. *Wrong* is climbing on fixtures in the bathroom. *Wrong* is leaving the yard and sidewalk. Right is anything you can get away with, including all of the above.

Manner of Discipline

To spank an infant is useless and very damaging. The child has no real concept of wrongdoing and cannot internalize right and wrong yet. To explain why something is wrong is also useless, and for the same reasons.

For most children younger than a year, a sharp "No!" can be enforced, if necessary, by picking up the child and redirecting him or her. This is a powerful symbolic action, this changing of the child's position and direction. *Not there. Here. Not that. Something else.*

If the child persists, divert him or her with a toy or a new thing to see and do.

Analyzing the Method's Success

Let's look at two imaginary mommies, Anna and Zelda. Each has a child six months old. Both respond promptly to their babies' cries, answering needs quickly as best they can. Both have children who are well on their way to developing an excellent basis of trust in human beings.

Today, Anna puts her baby down for a nap at noon after a feeding. Normally her baby sleeps for three hours in the afternoon. Today she wakes up crying at 1 P.M.

Now it happens that the wise old grandmother is over for a visit. "What time does the baby usually get up from her nap?" she asks.

The young mother looks at the clock. "Usually not until three." She starts to get up. "I'll go check on her."

"That baby's got you wrapped around her little finger. It's good to let her cry a little. Exercises her lungs. And lets her know she's not the only one in the world. Leave her be. She'll fall back to sleep eventually," the well-meaning grandmother advises. After all, she raised half a dozen kids back when you had to haul water and stoke a woodstove.

Anna sits back down. She tries to ignore the wails from the back of the house. Finally, after a nerve-wracking hour, she checks on her sobbing, gulping infant.

Following Grandmother's advice, she practices this same tactic for several days. Now when she puts her baby in the crib, it takes her an hour to get the child settled for her nap. The baby doesn't seem to want to go into her crib anymore. Nap time becomes more and more difficult.

The baby, you see, now associates her crib with loneliness and abandonment. Her mother does not respond when she needs her anymore. Her sleep pattern has changed and she no longer gets the cuddling she needs. That foundation of trust is eroding.

And what are the results for Anna? She has inadvertently made more work and stress for herself. Out of it all she has a fussier baby.

Meanwhile, there's Zelda, who also has a wise old grandmother who advises Zelda not to spoil her infant by catering to the child's whims. Zelda puts her son down for a nap as usual at noon. But the boy wakes up at 12:45. Zelda picks him up and does all the mother things: checking his diaper, burping him, cuddling and singing to him. She lays him down. Fifteen minutes later, he starts crying again.

She goes back in. "What's the matter, Sweetie?" she asks, "Are you lonely?"

She ignores the laundry piles in the hallway and sits in the rocking chair, rocking her son back and forth and talking to him. Thirty minutes later, he falls asleep and sleeps for one hour.

The next day, she lays her son down to sleep at noon and he wakes up at 1 P.M. She decides he's simply changed his sleeping habits and gets him up. He goes back for a nap at three and sleeps two hours until dinner. When he wakes up, he spends a half hour cooing and babbling in his crib until he cries for his mother.

Zelda has made less work and more time for herself by promptly responding to her son's needs as he communicates them.

The examples are a bit overblown, but the principle, I hope, is clear. Before age one year, children who are pampered, whose demands are answered consistently, are generally happier and easier to tend.

So why did Anna listen to Grandmother anyway? Because Grandmother carries the authority of age and experience. Grandmother is actually a very important person to listen to and can dispense important information across the generations. But Grandmother's advice, and anyone else's (including mine!), must be tested in two ways.

1. Does it work?
2. Is it logical for my child?

Anna's grandmother's advice did not work, and its logical conclusion was to make Anna's baby reluctant to be left alone. Had Anna noticed right away that things were getting worse, she could have reversed her policy and gotten her baby back to a better comfort level with a minimum of fuss. Note, though, that the situation arose from a natural change in sleep patterns, something a parent cannot alter or change back again.

What about the pounds and pounds of advice both Anna and Zelda receive from well-meaning friends and relatives other than their grandmothers? The same tests apply. But there is a third test as well:

3. Why am I listening to this advice?

The answer could be, "So other people will think I'm a good parent." For the child's sake, that's never the right answer.

Ruth, incidentally, was very susceptible to others' perceptions of her. She wanted to give her girls every good thing because as a child she herself had been too often neglected and denied the good things. But even more, she wanted to be viewed as a parent who was good to her children. She put that need—a very personal one—above her children's true need for consistent discipline. In essence she became a "bad" parent in order to look like a "good" one.

Of course I use "bad" and "good" in vernacular context. She was not bad. Misled, yes. Perhaps confused as to her role, no doubt. But in her mind's eye she held her children's best interests dear. That is not being a bad parent.

An infant cannot distinguish between "wants" and "needs." Everything the child asks for is wanted and therefore needed. A baby younger than one year has no separate identity with which to want things for himself or herself in the same sense we older folks do. There is no self yet.

Until that magical split comes between baby and caregiver, and with it the magical melding of bad Mommy and good, bad Baby and good, there are only needs.

That all changes in this action-packed second year. As Baby learns to get about on knees and then legs, as the child becomes a person apart from Mommy and Daddy, wants become separate from needs. The rules have changed. It's a brand-new ball game.

Discipline Now—This Year

"Highhhhh-*Hup!*" He knows his mission, this military drill sergeant. He's going to shape real men out of flabby boys. Every recruit standing rigidly at attention before him is convinced that compared to their sergeant, Genghis Khan was a wimp.

He begins his commentary on their value by denigrating them, excoriating them, berating them. "You @#$&* bunch of lazy, @#$%&* no-goods." And on and on and on.

He continues his evaluation of their worth as human beings by finding every tiny detail that is the least bit out of line: a smudge on a boot, an unbuttoned pocket, a twitch or flinch.

He concludes his appraisal by prescribing the medicine that will turn these cowardly, scatter-brained, selfish, undisciplined weaklings into the pride of a nation—liberal doses of running, push-ups, drills, demeaning chores, lots of cleaning, and an occasional surprise inspection.

This is more or less the kind of firm, no-nonsense

discipline Walt Raines wanted to bestow upon his errant Brendan.

Except it's not firm. It's just plain rigid. And whereas rigid discipline is fine for a bunch of adults being welded into an effective fighting force, it never, ever works on a living, growing child. It allows no room for growth.

Rigidity Versus Firmness

A child of four cannot cross the street without a parent. A child of six needs some help, as from a crossing guard. The child of ten handles traffic safely. That's growth. If you hold the six-year-old to the four-year-old's rules, the sixer will not learn to survive in traffic. The rigid rule, "You can only cross the street if Mommy or Daddy helps you," must be changed so the six-year-old's traffic skills can mature properly. That's flexibility.

And through all this, the wise parents draw the line and maintain it. The four-year-old is *never* allowed out in traffic. The six-year-old *must* have help from someone older. The ten-year-old had better be very careful and attentive. That's firmness.

Adjusting the Touch

A tennis instructor teaching a couple to play pairs tennis may use a rope. Tie one end of the rope around one partner's waist and the other end around the other's. If the instructor wants them to work about eight feet apart, he leaves eight feet of slack line between them. If he wants them to work ten feet apart, ten feet of rope separate them. Then they learn to move together, playing the balls sent their way while neither crowding each other nor leaving a gap in the middle of the court.

Picture firmness and flexibility as if they were that pair of tennis players, moving in concert, neither of them dominating, neither crowding the other.

For example: A one-year-old cannot negotiate stairs safely. Firmness says, "No, you cannot. We'll put the gate up to keep you from falling." Later, flexibility says, "You're four months older now, and getting pretty good at controlling your movements. You can climb on the stairs with me here helping."

Firmness says, "But don't go up without someone holding your hand. Later, flexibility says, "Your second birthday is close, and you can climb stairs well now by yourself."

Developing a style of combining firmness with flexibility is, by exact analogy, trying to hit a rapidly moving target. Your child is changing so quickly during toddlerhood that you must watch behavior and habits closely for clues of how to proceed. This is easier if you keep the goals of discipline in mind.

Goals of Discipline

One of a child's main tasks during this second year of life is learning what can be done and what cannot be done. Another task is learning how best to do what can be done. The foundation of intelligence, the ability to figure things out, is laid during this second year.

Your toddler at first uses random physical acts to gain a desired end. Some work; some don't. It's a shotgun approach. As sophistication grows, the child learns to stop and think about what to do before doing it. *Let's try this approach; it worked before. Forget that idea. It flubbed last time.*

This major transition from randomness to thoughtfulness will alter the effectiveness of discipline. Until the child begins considering actions, discipline is actually rote conditioning. When the child does such-and-so, the parent responds like this. Cause, effect. It's really quite effective in managing behavior . . .

Until individuation begins. Now pleasing Mommy and Daddy does not come automatically. Now we are going to test Mommy and Daddy as a means of clarifying our separate identity.

However, managing behavior is not the best or most important goal. When you're training a dog, behavior is all you're interested in. When you're training a child, you want that child to learn right from wrong and internalize the lessons.

The goal ultimately is to build a clear conscience in a youngster so that he or she does what is smart and right by choice whether or not you are present to enforce the child's behavior. Discipline, no longer mere behavior management, becomes an art.

You can point toward this goal in a toddler, but you cannot achieve it yet. What you will do is to prepare the child by imposing a system of right and wrong from without. If that system is fairly and equitably enforced, the child will adopt it by degrees until it is working on the child from the inside.

From the conditioned response *If I do this wrong thing, Mommy and Daddy will discipline me* comes, about the time the child enters school, an internalized response to temptation: *This is a wrong thing to do. I'd better not do it.*

Although success lies years in the future, the road begins here. An entitled child will never internalize the values system. The entitled child will always be ready to do whatever he or she can get away with. Oh, what grief that invites!

Methods of Discipline

Redirection and diversion will still work with the one- to two-year-old . . . sometimes. Maturity, though, has wised the child up. He or she now knows what Mommy and Daddy are doing—trying to get the child to forget about the forbidden act. Redirection and diversion work only if the kid lets them. Usually, the easy child does.

Working with the Easy Child
Marsha Jasper had no idea how lucky she had it. Her Brian was such an amenable little kid, always ready to embark on another adventure with Daddy, fairly good about cooperating with Mommy in matters of eating and behavior.

Tom and Marsha didn't think about it as such, but they were smoothing Brian's way to independence by letting him do for himself as much as possible. And that's a good ploy.

Give the Child Avenues for Independence. Brian was allowed to help dress himself, even though he usually botched the job. Brian was allowed to climb into his carseat himself even though it took longer than if someone lifted him into it. Brian helped Daddy wash the car and water the lawn. Daddy would lift Brian high so that he could pick an apple off the tree out back when Daddy could more easily pick the apple for him.

Brian was so wrapped up in doing new things that he felt no real need to test his parents. Certainly he opposed and tested from time to time. All children do as they emerge during this age. But it wasn't a rending experience for either Brian or his parents.

This is diversion of a sort. Tom and Marsha were channeling Brian's energies into other interests—in a real way, diverting him from possible trouble into other, happier pursuits.

Read Your Child. Marsha and Tom scored quite a coup when they realized that Brian's temper tantrums were actually frustration tantrums. It's a lot easier to deal rationally and gently with an outburst of frustration than with a display of anger. For everyone except the participant, the emotional energy level isn't nearly as high.

What do you want to read regarding your child's behavior? How about:

_____ Worst time of day for oppositional behavior?

_____ Best time of day for happy moods, peace?

_____ Changing patterns of sleep and play during the last few days? (Yes, they change that fast. Monitor closely.)

_____ What happens if the child is up late?

_____ What happens if the child goes to bed early?

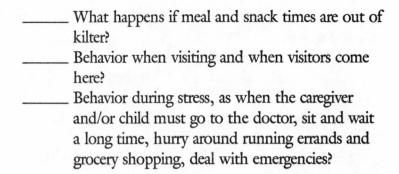

_____ What happens if meal and snack times are out of kilter?

_____ Behavior when visiting and when visitors come here?

_____ Behavior during stress, as when the caregiver and/or child must go to the doctor, sit and wait a long time, hurry around running errands and grocery shopping, deal with emergencies?

Knowing these things, you can *to an extent* program your life and your child's to minimize friction, surly behavior, irritations, and other factors that go with a need for tighter discipline. When they occur, you can realize that there are contributing factors other than the situation itself—lack of sleep, upset routine, whatever. It does not excuse the behavior, but it makes the behavior more understandable.

Now go down that list again and think about your own behavior. There are at least two personalities in the equation, the child's and the caregiver's. If either one is out of sorts, the other gets the fallout. Your child's misbehavior may be the fruit of your own short temper. Kids blot up other people's moods very quickly and well.

Use Redirection and Diversion As a First Choice. Give the methods of babyhood discipline a chance to work first before moving on to stronger efforts. They are gentlest.

Limit Corporal Punishment. Consider this scenario: Brian, now aged twenty months, and Marsha are visiting at Carrie's house. Brian heads for a freestanding globe he is not allowed to touch.

Brian reaches for it with smeary little fingers.

Marsha sternly rebukes him. "No, Brian!"

He persists.

She picks him up and sets him down elsewhere.

He returns to it.

She again redirects him and offers him a bright plastic toy—a diversion.

He drops the toy and returns to the forbidden activity.

He's pushing her. She knows it. He knows it. She redirects him. He turns on his heel to head right back there. She gives him a single gentle swat on the diaper.

The unexpected response startles him and frightens him. He cries lustily. She sets him on her lap and offers the toy. She has won, but she's not making him feel like a loser.

Marsha's use of corporal punishment possessed these desirable features:

1. It was gentle and brief. It frightened rather than hurt.

2. It was *not* done in anger.

3. It was a last resort.

4. It was repeatable. Had Brian persisted, she would have persisted.

5. It was consistent. Leaving that globe alone was a rule Brian knew about. He knew where the line was, and he knew Marsha would not let him cross it.

"Wait," you cry. "I don't think it was the last resort at all. There were other tactics Marsha should have tried first."

Quite possibly so. Every person's style differs. The Yorks, for example, refused to use any corporal punishment whatever on their Kevin. No matter the method and style, the five points listed should pertain. It must be gentle, brief, not connected in any way with anger, repeatable, and consistent.

Disciplining the Difficult Child

"Difficult child? She certainly is!" Jenny paused in her analysis of Sara. "Not bad, just stubborn and cranky."

Sara and others like her require everything Brian would get, but in megadoses. Jenny might be watching Sara very closely for clues as to Sara's thoughts, intents, and moods. Observation teaches much indeed. Jenny ought to divert Sara's energies diligently, as much as possible. Go places, do things, allow her freer rein to explore and express her independence. Discipline must be administered fairly and with unflagging firmness. Sara needs even more unconditional loving than does Brian. Brian already basks in positive feedback. Sara needs more.

One of the reasons Sara got along much better with Jenny than with Grandma is that Grandma was intent upon shaping Sara into a particular preconceived notion of what Sara ought to be (essentially, a miniature Jenny). Jenny, with no preconceptions, accepted Sara for what she was.

That is an important key. Is your child difficult intrinsically? Or does a large proportion of the difficulty come because the child is not exactly the way you intended?

Consider the matter carefully. Watch your child. Pick out strengths and weaknesses, preferences, mannerisms, habits. The whole child is hanging out there naked at this age, unable to hide feelings and preferences. What you see is what you got.

Sara was impatient and cranky. To some degree, she always would be. Grandma fought those tendencies in vain.

Sara was obstinate. To some degree, she always would be. Grandma butted heads with her in vain.

Sara could change those tendencies somewhat as she approached adulthood if she decided to. Grandma would not change them. If Sara were not such a strong personality, Grandma might be able to beat those tendencies down and shove them underground as it were. But Grandma would not be changing them. They would emerge sooner or later, drastically altered perhaps, but there.

Kevin, on the other hand, was past being difficult. Kevin was dangerous.

The Yorks, you recall, had a real problem on their hands whether or not they chose to accept Mrs. Foran's word on it. Somehow, they had to teach Kevin not to murder.

Kevin illustrates the window of opportunity I so often mention. At age eighteen months, Kevin could be helped with a minimum of work. At two and a half, he would be turned around only with difficulty. And past three, the window would essentially close. Turning around after that age will still be possible, but it will be very difficult. There is always hope, but avoiding blood, sweat, and tears is always preferable. After the third-year window closes, Kevin's behavior might be modified in other ways, primarily disciplinary methods external to himself, but he would have lost his best chance to begin internalization of right and wrong. How? By not having a solid code of right and wrong imposed upon him from without.

Mrs. York was certain that Kevin was too young to know right from wrong and that when he asked for something, he needed it.

That is true of an infant. It is not true now. What Kevin needs most at this stage of life is narcissistic wounding, and Mr. and Mrs. York have been minimizing that.

While in one way she was pursuing a style more appropriate to a very small child, in another way Mrs. York was using a style appropriate to a much older one. She took a great deal of effort to explain to Kevin why his actions of the moment were wrong. Unfortunately, a toddler doesn't give a rip. Doesn't remember. Doesn't benefit from wordy explanations. Explanations are for older children whose thinking is firmer and more sophisticated.

Mrs. York's discipline and correction, then, were doubly inappropriate and therefore essentially ineffectual.

Let us assume now that Mrs. York decided she was indeed harboring a nascent serial killer and wanted to turn things around immediately. It was a good time to do so, while that window of opportunity still yawned open.

She would do essentially what any thoughtful parent ought to do, but she would have to hew the line more insistently and firmly. These following points apply to all children generally; they must apply to an entitled child stringently.

Set Clear Limits. First and foremost, Kevin must know what he is allowed to do and what he is not allowed to do. Part of the boundaries civilization sets delineates how much a person is allowed to encroach on others' physical and emotional space. That is Kevin's biggie. He has absolutely no inkling (rather, he refuses to accept or think about it) that his right to swing his fist stops short of the next person's nose.

The next Sunday morning, Mrs. Foran and Shauna winced as Kevin came through the door again with his angelic face and lethal outlook. But they were ready for him this time.

Mrs. Foran scooped him up the moment his mommy left. He was still wailing as she addressed him nose to nose. "In this room, Kevin, no child ever, *ever* strikes another one. If you try to hit anyone at all, you'll be sent to a crib like a little baby. Understood?"

Further wailing blurred Kevin's response.

Within a minute, he took a swing at Jason with a truck. Shauna pounced, catching him in time. She swept him up and toted him upside down over to a baby crib. He was left there, with Shauna nearby, for ten minutes as he howled. Ten minutes is a long time to a little child, remember. (It's also a long time for nursery workers to listen to that racket.)

She lifted him out, hugged him, warned him never ever to hit anyone, and turned him loose to play.

Did that cure him? Certainly not. He must have been in and out of that crib half a dozen times. Like an errant hockey player, he spent most of his time in the penalty box.

Mrs. Foran had drawn a clear line. She enforced it. She did not work much on other rules. They would come later. This was the big one, the most important one, and she tackled it first.

At home, Mrs. York must similarly set clear limits and then adhere to those boundaries.

Be Firm and Consistent. At the nursery, Kevin encountered the two forms of consistency that are essential for discipline at this or any other age.

1. The rules are enforced consistently by everyone. Shauna put him in the slammer. Mrs. Foran put him in the slammer. At home, Mr. and Mrs. York would have to work out an agreement by which they both provided the same consistent discipline. It would do no good for Mrs. York to enforce a rule if Mr. York let it slide. To present a united front, the Yorks must follow a two-fold plan: Neither parent may ever contradict the other in front of Kevin. Any discussion or disagreement should be held in private, away from the child's ears and eyes. And discussion should occur frequently enough for the rules to be consensual all the time.

2. The enforcer is consistent. Mrs. York would have to carefully follow through every single time. She could not enforce a rule one time and let it slide the next. Mrs. Foran was oak-solid in this regard.

Admit When You Are Wrong. Even a child approaching two years old is developing a well-honed sense of fair play. If Mrs. York catches herself correcting Kevin unfairly—that is, accusing him or punishing him for something he didn't do—apologies are in order.

For a child like Brian, who really does get along well,

apology is all the more important. A sense of fairness, or at least justice, both helps the child feel he or she is appreciated as an individual and makes the rules less onerous. Most important of all, it models an immensely important truth you will want the child to practice later—it is okay to admit you're wrong. It's all right to apologize.

To Kevin and Brian, yes, and Sara, too, parents *are* perfect. Apology will not damage that veneer of perfection. Parental perfection is not based upon the parents' qualities but upon the child's stage in life. You can err, and you can say you're sorry. It makes no difference to your image before your child.

Knock It Off with the Verbose Explanations. Patient explanations dull the effectiveness of a disciplinary moment by dragging it out beyond the child's interest span. Toddlers live moment to moment, and what was significant a moment ago is no longer of import. Discipline must also possess that quality of being virtually immediate and yet still well-thought-out. But "instantaneous," or nearly so, does not mean "capricious." It means "prompt."

Mrs. Foran did not explain. She stated the rule in one short sentence and meted the punishment. *That* Kevin could understand.

The day is soon coming—in a few years or so—when explanations will be in order. Internalization of conscience then will benefit from explanations. As children develop some sophistication in thinking of abstracts—about when they start school—they will not only be able to grasp explanations but insist upon them.

In his mid-teens, Brendan Raines had fully mastered

abstraction. That is, he could talk theories, discuss nonmaterial matters, and experience a sensation vicariously. He could read or hear about something and imagine it with some degree of accuracy. Driving a race car around the track at Daytona, for example—he probably would never actually do that, but he could pretty well imagine what it would be like. The small child cannot do any of that.

Discipline for Brendan, then, can be remarkably sophisticated. It should never involve corporal punishment. At his age, physical retribution would not serve the purpose of deterring behavior and would correctly be construed as a sign that the parent still considers him a small child.

Just like the eighteen-month-old Brian, Brendan the teen hungers for independence and yet is not quite up to handling it, at least not completely. He fears it also in a way. Walt will do well to offer Brendan the same opportunity for growth that Brian is getting—a gradual expansion of privileges with the chance that Brian, or Brendan, might fall.

Both kids must be allowed to fail while it is still safe to do so. From failure and mistakes come wisdom, be it teen or mini-teen. Explanations do just fine for Brendan.

All the children, from one on up, can benefit from positive discipline.

Positive Discipline

Corporations, celebrities, and politicians spend many, many dollars on "spin doctors." A spin doctor finds the best and most positive way of looking at a really messy situation.

Example: The politician boasts, "I saved the taxpayers ten thousand dollars by trimming certain expenditures." That's the positive spin. The negative side not mentioned is: "I also cost the taxpayers twenty million dollars when I let a crucial error slip by."

The taxpayer may understandably look askance at such shenanigans, but they work quite well when dealing with small children. Positive discipline is nothing more than putting a positive spin on requests and demands in order to minimize negatives.

You engage positive discipline in two ways. One is to arrange the child's environment in such a way as to be able to minimize no-no's.

Leave a stack of dispensable magazines on the table for the child to leaf through, fling about, possibly tear. Put breakable and dangerous kitchenware in upper cabinets so the child can explore lower ones safely. Some things will ever and always be no-no's, such as the globe at Carrie's. That is as it should be. We are talking about minimizing, not eliminating.

At this age, play without purpose is a particularly valuable growth tool. In fact there is no such thing at this age as play without purpose. What seems like random play to an observer is actually rife with purpose as the child works out the rules and physical laws of life. Try to minimize no-no's during this important random play. Mud puddles? Great! Let the child go for it. Kids are washable. Stomping water, making mud pies, swishing, feeling, splattering— such tactile learning stretches the imagination, and it's just plain fun. You can deny the child all that, a negative reaction, or you can start running the bathwater (another delicious tactile experience, baths!). Guess which way I vote?

The other way to build positive discipline is simply to recast requests and commands from negative to positive phrasing. I offer this caveat: Don't make it a request ("Would you like to . . . ?"). When you get a negative response you're stuck. For example: Instead of saying, "Don't touch that electrical cord!" say "Let's play with this string of beads instead." Not: "Wouldn't you rather play with this string of beads?"

Instead of "You can't play in the bathroom," say, "Let's play in the living room where I can watch while I fold the clothes."

Instead of: "Don't interrupt Mommy while she's on the phone," say "You must wait a minute until I'm done talking to your grandma. Then we'll read that book."

Of course once the promise is made it must be honored.

Along the same vein, you'll find it beneficial to recognize the child's positive behaviors. Parents too often don't do this nearly enough anyway.

Emphasize Positive Behavior Rather Than Negative

Misbehaviors, especially repetitive ones, may be done to gain attention. You already know the child's credo, that negative attention is better than no attention at all. Giving luxuriant praise for positive behavior provides your child with less need to misbehave.

Consider this tactic a breath of fresh air. As a society, we gloss over the positive and focus on the negative. There is that element within us that dwells gleefully upon tragedy—watching the Indy 500 in anticipation of a really awful crash, hanging on every word regarding the latest weird or gruesome crime, gasping over floods and earthquakes. Your child shares that fascination with horror, although in a different context; for example, the child has no real grasp of death. Children, though, dwell on mistakes, on slights, on injustices. On the negative. Invariably. Tell a child nine wonderful things right with him and one thing wrong, and he'll pick up on the wrong.

That's why *positivism* is so important—as a counter to the inherent *negativism*. And yet, children hang upon any positive stroke you can give them—undiluted positive strokes.

It may therefore take some rethinking on your part. If your toddler performs a task you've asked him to do such as helping pick up his toys, make a big deal of it. "What a great helper you are. Now Mommy has more time to play with you or read you a story."

Not a bribe. Not a conditional love response. Praise.

There is another aspect of discipline I touched on under the heading "Socialization in Today's Cruel World" in Chapter 3. This is socialization in today's cruel world. Please do not teach your child to be compliant toward adults other than their parents. The so-called "well-behaved child" is exactly what the abductor or enticer is looking for, the child who obeys. Once upon a time, obedience was a virtue. No more.

Obedience to you, yes. Respect toward others, certainly. But obedience to others has disintegrated out of sheer necessity to yell and tell. It's the new reality.

It makes me sad.

The Biblical Roots of Discipline

"Spare the rod and spoil the child."

Boy, how many times have I heard that one! Fathers in my counsel use it all too frequently to justify the kind of rigidly authoritarian discipline that destroys children. They think they're being scriptural. Everyone is quick to quote it, but hardly anyone really thinks about it.

Here's another verse you've undoubtedly heard many times: "Thy rod and thy staff, they comfort me."

Same rod. This time it brings comfort, not corporal punishment. Not browbeating and denigration. Proverbs 22:15 calls it a "rod of correction," and that is exactly how shepherds used rods such as the rod spoken of in the Twenty-third Psalm. They corrected errant sheep with their rod, poking, prodding, changing the animals' direction, waving it—but almost never striking their charges.

And while we're on the subject, look at Proverbs 13:24: "He who spares his rod hates his son, / But he who loves him disciplines him promptly." *Spare* is more in the context of not responding immediately than of letting up on the correction too quickly.

There's not a whole lot in the Bible about child-rearing, and I can see that it's better so. We as a race are much inclined to adhere to the letter of a biblical rule rather than its heart. Jesus complained about that very thing in Mark 7. What little the Bible does provide is remarkably balanced. In Ephesians 6, Paul warns children to obey their parents and in the same breath warns parents not to frustrate their children, provoking them, angering them.

When Scripture gets specific, it often goes for the heart more than the head, for the whole child rather than the child's behavior. For example, over and over, our Lord asks that we teach our children history and tradition. Give them a sense of place in time and a basis for knowing God and wondering at His love. "Tell them the story."

Various races and nationalities delight in teaching their children about their roots. For instance, many men and women whose ancestors came from Africa find identity and comfort—and much pleasure—in African culture. Do Christian parents similarly immerse themselves in the history and culture of the faith?

That is the aspect of child-rearing the Bible emphasizes most. Let us hew to what is important and not seek a phrase here and a sentence there to support some pet philosophy.

Beginning a Spiritual Life

Can a child less than two years old understand stories? Certainly. The human heart is programmed in such a way that stories can impart truths that preaching cannot. I use stories all the time to reach young children.

For example, I will ask a young client to tell me a story. Children love to do that. Some tales sound pretty inane, if you measure them against the latest Oscar-winning film script. On the other hand, for passion and depth of meaning, no movie, however erudite, can match a small child's story. The child will usually tell a story about a person the kid's age with a problem much like the child's own grief. The ending will reflect the child's fantasy of being able to do something about the problem. On occasion during this day and age, machine guns enter into the solution.

Then I will say, "My turn," and I will tell a story. It will be virtually the same story, with the same kind of child, the same kind of problem. The only deviation will be the solution. I will end my story with a narrative of a workable, actual solution to the child's problem. No preaching, no discussion—no "nonfiction," if you will. The child grasps the alternative solution without either of us actually articulating it.

Small children, in fact, cannot understand and articulate abstracts. But below conscious level the messages of stories sink right in.

Stories, therefore, are your entrée into the child's spiritual growth, just as they were Jesus', just as they were for virtually all the characters described in the Old Testament. Even the Ten Commandments and the rules of Deuteronomy are couched within a story.

So read your child Bible storybooks. Choose those books carefully for content, that they reflect accurately the meanings of the stories of Scripture, for rest assured your child will pick up at least the rudiments. You want them to be the right rudiments, the clear foundation.

Reading Bible stories to your child does four magical things. Like any other reading, Bible-story reading:

• *Cements the bond between parent and child as nothing else can.* This is a one-on-one experience of the warmest and most intimate kind.

• *Instills as nothing else can a feeling of being loved.* As your child nestles in the safety of your lap, hearing your voice, your reading teaches, "I love you" quite apart from the story itself.

• *Improves the child's language skills.* Hearing at this age is quite as important as speaking. The child absorbs the cadence and beauty of the mother tongue, hears it correctly and clearly spoken. The story the child hears becomes a model for speaking.

• *Teaches spiritual fundamentals.* This is by far the most important of lessons you will impart to your little one. As your child approaches adulthood, he or she will question your faith and your values. This is very necessary. The child must move beyond blind acceptance of your faith and develop a viable faith of his or her own.

Right here at age one to two, you are laying the foundation. And you are giving a crucial message over and above the story: God is so important to you that you are sitting there telling about Him. You have just said more about God than any amount of preaching later can offer.

When the child enters school, Sunday schools will drift away from storytelling into games, puzzles, and fill-in-the-blank quizzes. But always, even as the child enters adulthood, the story will remain the teaching tool of choice. You cannot, even at this age, read and tell too many stories.

Be advised, incidentally, that miracles mean nothing to a one-year-old. Your child has no grasp of reality as opposed to fantasy or divine intervention. Supernatural and natural are the same thing at this age. Feed five thousand? No problem. Walk on water? No big thing. So you will not be trying to impress upon your child God's miraculous or divine nature. Your child will be learning that He loves His children, all of them. Your child will be learning that God is the most important thing in the world.

Sufficient lesson for a small child—and for us as well.

7. THE BUCK STOPS HERE

EPILOGUE

A wise son makes a glad father . . .

PROVERBS 10:1

So whaddaya think already?" Brendan Raines stomped down the kickstand on his brand-new motocross bike and stepped back.

His dad, the ex-Brooklynite, stared at it. "What's with this 'whaddaya-think-already' stuff? You think by speaking the correct English you'll talk me into it? You should live so long. What do I think? I think the state of Texas and Dr. Warren are conspiring to break your neck so I can collect your insurance, which is still in New York along with the smart money." Walt Raines circled the bike warily as a golfer circles his winning putt or a small child approaches a new and unusual food.

"Dad, you know what he said—whether or not we moved out here, we would've had this friction. He said all kids go through it some, and it woulda happened in New York too."

"Yeah, yeah, yeah. 'It's not Texas, it's the timing.' Bren, the man lives here. I should believe a resident? If he lived in Yonkers or even New Haven I'd believe him better when he says it's not Texas warping you. Right.

Like a plywood board in a winter rain." Walt curled his fingers up, a dramatic gesture, albeit overblown. "So you think you're gonna win trophies with this thing?"

"Yeah. I'm one of the youngest qualifiers in my division. All I need is for you should drive me and the bike down to Gonzales this weekend."

"Don't they teach you any better English than that in this hick school?"

"Dad, Irving is not a hick school. You have this weird fixation that unless a place has fourteen million people and a subway system, it's not a city." Brendan headed for the back door. Lunchtime. Almost.

Walt followed, with one last glance over his shoulder at that infernal bike. "So? Show me a place where the big team is named the Dallas Cowboys and I'll show you a hick town. Ever hear of the Brooklyn Cowboys? Does Rockefeller Plaza have a big herd of bronze horses running through its fountain? Can you get lost in Manhattan and end up in anyplace named Mesquite?"

"We wouldn't've got lost if you'd turned left when I told you to. I was reading the map right." Brendan led the way into the house.

The screen door slammed.

The Ultimate Lesson

Teenager and toddler. Two kids struggling to literally be somebody. This essentially adult exchange between Brendan and his dad reflects what an exchange between a toddler and the parent might reveal on a different scale.

Both teen and toddler are working on separation and individuation, the toddler at one end and the teen at the other. Walt could have started the process a decade earlier by doing what he was doing now.

Brendan's banter with his father was an excellent step forward in his own individuation. Over the last several months, they both learned to hear each other. They had at last become comfortable with each other. It was a first. Brendan learned that he could differ from his dad without being wrong. That was new. Walt had to learn the same lesson. That was even newer. For all Brendan's life, Walt's opinion had been the right one. Now they could tease each other, listen to each other, and come to know each other as adults for the first time.

To set the record straight, the state of Texas and I are not really conspiring to do Brendan in. I did not specifically urge Walt to buy him that bike. I recommended that Walt help Brendan develop a life of his own. What you will be doing with your toddler on a limited, intimate scale, Walt was doing with Brendan on an adult scale. He was helping him make adult friends of his own apart from his parents and helping him pursue interests of his own. Motocross happened to be the pursuit for which Brendan developed a keen interest. Frankly, I never would have thought of motocross myself. It did the job though.

Brendan followed a sport his father had never even heard of before coming to this "forsaken state," as Walt described Texas. Brendan succeeded brightly in it, too, not to please his father but to please himself.

Brendan had learned the ultimate lesson of separation and individuation:

**I am responsible to me.
My choices, ultimately, are my own.
The buck stops here.**

This is the lesson for which you must begin preparing your little child now. It is the lesson that will, more than anything else, help your child resist peer pressure toward foolishness and wrongdoing. Drugs? Alcohol? Immorality? The best defense is a strongly ingrained knowledge that *I am responsible for my actions.*

Teach your child what love is by loving your child. Teach your child what honesty is by being honest. And then, eventually, you will teach your child to stand up, sometimes alone and sometimes in a crowd, for what is right and to take the consequences for the choices made. Your primary instrument for teaching your child will not be the material in this book, although I trust you will find it helpful for understanding and dealing with this challenging age. Your primary instrument will be the relationship you forge with your child.

Relationship.

Did Walt take Brendan down to Gonzales? Yes. Did he win? Two firsts and a second. Was Walt proud? Absolutely. Was Brendan even prouder? Sure was. Incidentally, the nose and ear ornaments are a thing of the past. You don't wipe out comfortably in a full-face helmet with that hardware stuck all over your head.

Go the Extra Mile

Little Sara, just starting down the long road toward realizing that she would be responsible for her actions, will have a harder time traveling through life. In the next few years, she will be identified as having some attention deficit disorder problems. Jenny, her mom, will then have to explore different ways for Sara to cope with life, to learn, and to love. And yet, as she comes into maturity, Sara, too, will have to face the reality, *I am responsible for my actions. I will gain or lose according to my diligence in taking personal responsibility.* To help her, Jenny will make sacrifices to get Sara special schooling and special hands-on opportunities to learn.

Shauna Moore's Afton, deaf but particularly bright, will succeed in part because her mama, tough as nails, will provide backup and buffer. Afton faces an excellent future because she will come to know that her mama will make her get through life on her own and yet will never let her down.

Ruth's two girls will probably never learn that cardinal lesson. Sherry and Susan may learn coping mechanisms, and yes, if they want to get along easier in life they can make major improvements in their ability to relate to others. Ruth has gone many extra miles. She will go miles farther.

And Brian?

Away Down the Road

It is party animal Brian Jasper's second birthday. Standing behind him, his mom takes his right hand in her right hand, his left hand in her left, and deftly operates him, puppet-like, as he strikes the match to light his two birthday candles. He cackles in anticipation.

While the candles waver in the uncertain breeze, his friends sing happy birthday to him. It's pretty much the same gang as gathered back on his first birthday—mostly friends of his parents, older kids, and of course Dumkopf. But Brian is not the same kid.

His body shape is much different, his coordination much better, his life experiences vastly expanded, his language quite sophisticated. His favorite toy this time is a play board his dad can attach to his carseat or high chair. With a red plastic steering wheel, yellow plastic gearshift, mirror, beeping horn, and bell, it's as close as you can come to driving the Daytona course without being there. It's a much more advanced toy than that little plastic slide.

With his mom and dad behind him and before him, urging him along and leading the way, he will march away down the road to independence in fine style.

I invite you also to take your little one's hand and walk together down the road of life's great adventure. As enticing as the destination of adulthood may seem, getting there—you and your child together—will be more than half the fun.

God bless your journey.

ABOUT THE AUTHOR

Paul Warren, M.D., is a behavioral pediatrician and adolescent medicine specialist. He serves as medical director of the Child and Adolescent Division and the Adolescent Day Program of the Minirth Meier New Life Clinic in Richardson, Texas and also has an active outpatient practice. He also is a professional associate with the Center for Marriage and Family Intimacy based in Austin, Texas.

Dr. Warren received his M.D. degree from the University of Oklahoma Medical School. He completed his internship and residency at Children's Medical Center in Dallas, Texas where he also served as chief resident. He did a fellowship in behavioral pediatrics and adolescent medicine at the University of Texas Southwestern Medical School and Children's Medical Center in Dallas.

An expert in child and adolescent issues, Dr. Warren is a popular seminar speaker who addresses audiences nationwide and is a regular guest on the Minirth Meier New Life Clinic radio program. His other books include *Kids Who Carry Our Pain*, *The Father Book*, and *Things That Go Bump in the Night*.

Dr. Warren and his wife Vicky have a son, Matthew.